THE BOOK OF **SAKE**

THE BOOK OF SAKE

A Connoisseur's Guide

Philip Harper

WITH SAKE SELECTIONS BY Haruo Matsuzaki
FOREWORD Chris Pearce
PHOTOGRAPHY Mizuho Kuwata

KODANSHA INTERNATIONAL
Tokyo • New York • London

CONTENTS

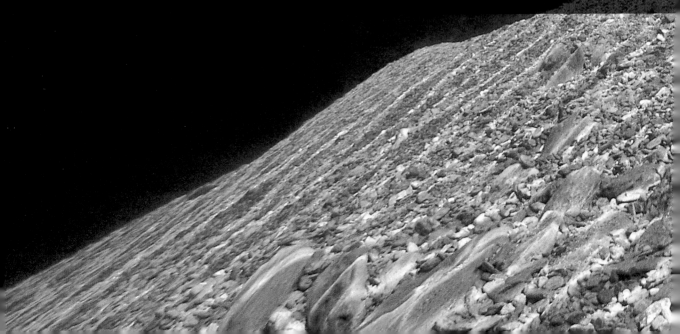

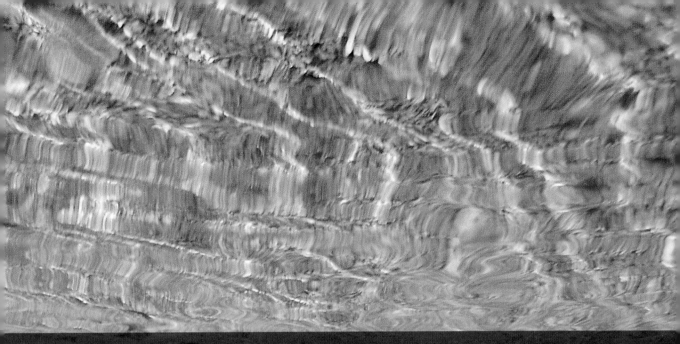

THIS PAGE: A detail of one of the traditional buildings in the Ozawa Shuzō brewery complex (page 63) on the outskirts of Tokyo.

NOTE: Japanese words are *italicized* on first mention and again in their defining section. A quick guide to Japanese pronunciation can be found on page 30.

Distributed in the United States by Kodansha America, Inc., and in the United Kingdom and continental Europe by Kodansha Europe Ltd.

Published by Kodansha International Ltd., 17–14 Otowa 1-chome, Bunkyo-ku, Tokyo 112–8652, and Kodansha America, Inc.

Text copyright © 2006 by Philip Harper. Design and line drawings copyright © 2006 by Kodansha International Ltd.
All rights reserved. Printed in Japan.
ISBN-13: 978–4–7700–2998–0
ISBN-10: 4–7700–2998–5

Library of Congress Cataloging-in-Publication Data available

First edition, 2006
15 14 13 12 11 10 09 08 07 06   10 9 8 7 6 5 4 3 2 1

www.kodansha-intl.com

Foreword

by Chris Pearce

Every night, in hundreds of restaurants and bars across America, you can see bemused patrons poring over the sake menu. They may not be sure which label to order—the information needed to make a sound choice has been in short supply—but there is no doubting their sincerity or desire. The amount of sake imported from Japan has doubled in the last eight years, as more and more people realize that sake represents, along with beer and wine, one of the world's three great families of fermented beverages. For many sake enthusiasts, just enjoying a favorite label is no longer enough: they want to move on to deeper knowledge of how sake is made, its regional characteristics, its history and brewing lore, its deep intertwinings with other areas of Japanese culture.

In the pages of this book Philip Harper offers himself as a cordial guide and companion, sharing hard-won knowledge gleaned from fourteen years among the vats at three small, highly respected breweries. Having advanced through the hoary sake apprentice system to the equivalent of senior management level, he gives us a unique perspective on the traditional sake world. While doing so he maintains a healthy British skepticism towards accepted truths, and crafts his own unique interpretation of what sake appreciation and enjoyment is all about.

A useful distinction is made between sake drinking ("about pleasure and nothing else") and sake tasting ("an attempt to gather as much information about the sake under consideration as possible"). Harper is obviously enamored of both approaches, and devotes a number of pages to the pairing of sake with traditional Japanese food as well as non-Japanese cuisines. But even more valuable are his translations of Haruo Matsuzaki's reviews of fifty different sakes from every region of Japan. Reading these reviews conveys better than anything else a sense of the interplay of creativity and tradition going on today as brewers strive to produce new and exciting labels for an ever more appreciative public.

Sake today is on the verge of a renaissance, not only in Japan but around the world. There are so many different styles, so many expressions achievable with variations in rice, water, and above all technique, that one could spend a lifetime exploring them, as in fact many people have. Philip Harper provides a much-needed window onto this wide world, sharing his knowledge, opening hidden doors, and through it all conveying his deep respect and affection for the tiny microorganisms whose efforts give human beings such contentment, joy, and inspiration.

Introduction

I first tasted sake when I came to Japan in 1988, and ever since have been drinking it with unflagging enthusiasm—and ever-deepening pleasure.

Although I immediately enjoyed the cozy sharing of hot sake in tiny cups with my new Japanese colleagues, like many sake fans, I first seriously became hooked when I was ambushed by the charms of the fine, fragrant sake called *ginjō*—served chilled, to my surprise.

However, in time, my focus changed to something called *nama*, with a peculiarly pithy zing and nutty notes that went through mesmerizing flavor shifts with the slightest change of temperature. I learned that sake is unpasteurized, and was so absorbed by it for a while that I paid little attention to anything else.

(Here we are, less than ten lines into this book, and a couple of Japanese words have surfaced. As I discovered early on, there are many styles of sake—and a host of strange-sounding words accompanying them. Many sake fans find the novel vocabulary part of the fun, but if you find it an obstacle, this book will help you sidestep them.)

In 1991, a surfeit of zeal persuaded me to join the staff of a small brewery. As a result, I have had the honor of spending the past fourteen winters in the company of many fine veteran craftsmen—and a few hardy women. I have found that a traditional brewery is a society-within-a-society, with its own quirks, customs, and superstitions. Sake has been made for centuries by guilds of seasonally active artisans, and you shall find something about the symbiotic relationship in the chapter on sake and regions.

Sake brewing goes most smoothly when the temperature in the brewery is about three notches too low for people to feel comfortable, but working in that environment gave me a renewed, visceral appreciation for the heartwarming pleasure of good sake served heated. The range of temperatures at which sake can be enjoyed give it an extra dimension. A great deal of sake is drunk warm—as its makers intended—but a lot of high-grade sake is made specifically to

be savored chilled. Temperature is important: a sake at its ideal temperature is reborn at a heightened level of deliciousness. Miss that spot, and even great sake may show you no more than mediocrity.

In my workplace, I discovered sake brewing to be as complicated and fascinating as it is exhausting. One does not have to know how one's tipple is made to enjoy it, but the Japanese system for converting rice to a delicious intoxicant has many features that make it intriguing. Moreover, there is an undeniable satisfaction in knowing some of the processes that give your favorite sake its special identity. Similarly, a sense of the history that has culminated in your mouthful of pleasure can give the enjoyment of sake extra spice.

The roots of sake go all the way back to Japan's mythical origins. The earliest chronicles, dating back almost 1,300 years, relate how an intrepid deity tricked a slavering, eight-headed monster into swallowing so much sake (eight vats full, one for each head) that it was unable to swallow the young lady who was next on the menu. There is not enough space in this book to discuss the history of sake at length, but those interested in how sake is made will find a few historical tidbits in the chapter entitled "The Brewer's Craft."

Returning to the subject of my early experiences, I can say that after my nama phase, and partly because of my interest in warm sake, I found myself increasingly preoccupied with the rich, earthier flavors that emerge as sake ages. For a few years, my conviction that aged, pasteurized sake represented the apotheosis of the sake experience was something for which I would have been prepared to fight to the death—always assuming that I could have found someone with similarly intemperate enthusiasm to accompany me.

I also found myself taken—no, *smitten*—with a traditional style called *yamahai*, which is profound of flavor and has an extra dimension to its acidity. Then, each fall, I have been infatuated anew with the gamboling flavors of new sake, fresh from the press. Now, after seventeen years of intensive and dedicated research, I can reveal for the first time the style of sake that is really the finest, most delicious and genuine: all of them.

As a fringe benefit of the hedonistic enjoyment of Japan's national drink, I have found it to be a key to many doors on the tapestry of Japanese life and ideas. For centuries, Japanese garden designers have used a technique called *shakkei* to give their creations a breathtaking scale and impact beyond what is physically possible in the limited space of any given site. Shakkei, meaning borrowed landscape, works by weaving the external natural landscape into the view of the garden as a backdrop. In the same manner, the names of sake brands hint at the wider reaches of Japanese culture, while the delights of sake itself are amplified by the panoramas of Japanese history, food, and ceramics. It is my hope that the reader will catch a glimpse of these grand vistas in the pages that follow.

Sake aging in bottles. Time is one key ingredient influencing the flavor of sake.

chapter One

Making the Most of Sake

Japanese magnolia. Enjoying whatever flowers are in bloom is one of the seasonal pleasures of Japanese life. Flower-viewing revelries are not complete without sake—a drink affectionately referred to as *hanami-zake*.

This book should help fan that spark of interest you have in sake. If you are already ablaze with enthusiasm, these pages should provide excellent fuel to stoke the fire.

I find myself hesitating at the outset, unsure of where to begin, because there are so many ways of thinking about sake—and enjoying it. A Japanese proverb tells us that there are ten colors for ten people, and you will get the most pleasure from sake when you find your own color. I know people who live for regional color—who are passionate about the sake of their ancestral home, or captivated by the charisma of sake from a specific area.

You may find yourself joining the ranks of the many sake fans who swoon for the zest of young, green, unpasteurized brews, or the rather less numerous (but no less vociferous) devotees of the funky amber-to-umber delights of aged sake. There are sake acolytes who worship a specific yeast, and others who are devoted to a certain rice variety. Likewise, there are devotees of individual breweries, and even individual brewers have their admirers. Of the many styles of sake, one may prove to be the one that takes root in your heart, subtly changing the hue of your life in the process.

◄ Whether fresh and fruity, fat and full-bodied, or funky and aged, sake offers an array of options for aperitifs, a meal-time libation, and after-dinner refreshment.

So, where to start? Early drafts of this book began by explaining all the different categories of sake, but, on less than sober reflection, it seemed more fun to start with ingestion rather than definition. Thus, we plunge right into the actual business of drinking, tasting, and eating with sake. Should mention of a particular sake style whet your interest, follow the page references and jump ahead. And I recommend you have a glass of sake in hand as you read.

▶ Grated daikon topped with salmon roe. A refreshing dish, excellent with lighter sake, such as a crisp, unpasteurized junmai ginjō.

THE SECRET OF SUCCESS
Finding the Ideal Temperature

Sake is fabulous over a wide range of temperatures. I personally survive the sweaty trials of the Japanese summer with the help of strong and spicy *genshu* (see page 44), served over ice. At the end of a bitter winter day in a freezing brewery, I am revived by good, workaday sake, warmed to thaw the chill in my bones. Somehow, I find there are persuasive reasons to enjoy sake at all the temperatures in between, too. Finding the sweet spot for the particular sake you are drinking will double your pleasure.

On the Rocks

Potent undiluted genshu is safest for drinking over ice, but even ordinary sake (with about 15 to 16 percent alcohol) can be interesting. However, only well-balanced sake survives this diluting.

If you try it and your drink does not lose its character, you know you have found a well-made, versatile sake, and a delightful, refreshing warm-weather tipple into the bargain. Apart from the invigorating pick-me-up effect, it is endlessly fascinating to follow the shifts in flavor balance as ice melts in the sake. I find the spicy zest of unpasteurized sake particularly beguiling when presented this way. The drawback of sake on the rocks is that you do get purists looking sourly at you. A small price to pay, I believe.

Chilled Sake

Sake chilled to between 40° and 50° F (5° and 10° C) is called *reishu*. Top-grade *dai ginjō* (see page 40) is almost always served in this range. Most are crisp and light, and some lose definition when the temperature rises. The admission price to the elite world of dai ginjō is paid for (some might say paid through) the nose. Heat this type of sake, and you lose its delicate, costly bouquet. On the other hand, *over*-chilling will lock in those fragrances. Very fragrant sake benefits from moderate chilling, whatever the rank, since the aromatics can become fuzzy and cloying near room temperature. The same goes for the boisterous, green aromas of unpasteurized sake, so *nama-zake* (see page 42) is almost invariably served well chilled. Crisp, light, dry sake of all grades is good cold, though many in this style can work well at room temperature, too.

Chilled ginjō sake is excellent in glass cups or even wine glasses.

Low-alcohol sake tends to be on the sweet side, with well-above-average acidity balancing the flavor. Almost all the low-alcohol sakes are intended by their makers to be drunk cold, and who are we to demur?

A glance at the flavor chart (see pages 25–26) will show that categories on the left side blossom particularly well at low temperatures. The rule of thumb: if it is light, fruity, fragrant, and fresh, enjoy it cold.

Room Temperature

The equivalent in Japanese of the expression room temperature is *jō-on*, which means something similar to "normal temperature." Both generally mean somewhere between 60° and 70° F (15° and 20° C). Sakes with lots of body, flavor, and astringency are often at their best in this range. Astringency and bitterness that seem abrasive in a cold sake often melt into a luxuriant balance as the sake warms. A lot of pure-rice sakes do especially well at these temperatures. The majority of aged sakes also begin to come into their own around here, though there are lighter examples that also do fine chilled.

The less flowery, more ricey, earthy style of *ginjō* and *junmai ginjō* (pages 38) and the bulk of *honjōzō* brews (page 37) are well suited to drinking at room temperature. Though I have focused on the higher grades of sake, here is a good place to remember the others. Most cheaper (There: I've said it!) regular sake is intended to be drunk either heated or at room temperature. Many people who drink it do so every day, and its greatest virtue (apart from being cheap) is flexibility; good examples often work at a wide range of temperatures, but particularly at room temperature and above. This reflects the historical role of these workaday brews, treasured companions in daily life before refrigerators ever arrived in Japanese kitchens.

Hire-zake: Fugu-Fin Sake

Hire is the Japanese word for fin. *Hire-zake* is sake containing the toasted fin of a blowfish (*fugu*), which imparts a pleasant smoky flavor. The sake is served warm. The dried fin is toasted over a flame to release the flavor, then set in hot, regular sake to allow the smoky richness to permeate the brew. Although there are a few bottled examples of this sake on sale, it is more common to find *izakaya* and other restaurants preparing the sake on request.

From about this range up, the heavy guns of the *kimoto/yamahai* (page 43) genre also begin to show their best. When cold, they sometimes have a slightly grainy mouth feel, which diminishes toward room temperature and turns to ambrosia when lightly warmed. Their bitter or astringent flavors, which can be distracting or plain unpleasant at low temperatures, combine lusciously with sweet and tangy elements as the temperature rises.

Warm and Hot Sake

The Japanese word for heated sake is *kanzake*, and it is usually referred to by the abbreviated honorific form *o-kan*. Heated sake spans a wider spectrum of temperatures than that recommended for the two other categories, running from 85° to 130° F (30° to 55° C). The two ranges most often ordered are *nuru-kan* and *atsu-kan*—which are, respectively, the warm and the piping hot varieties. You may also come across the evocatively named *hito-hada* (literally, a person's skin)—which refers to sake heated to body temperature.

I go through crates of reviving, hot sake in the winter, and crisp, cold reishu in the summer. Mellow sake, served as is, is a staple in my house all year round. But for true, life-enhancing gustatory pleasure, gently warmed sake is king—if not the entire royal family. Drinking o-kan sake at this temperature offers an indescribable element of physical satisfaction and comfort related to the fact that this is *body* temperature. Consider the undoubted pleasure of taking a huge gulp of icy beer on a very hot day: this is by way of a restorative—an antidote to the heat. On a cold winter's night, the warmth of a well-brewed o-kan sake induces a feeling of well being that is both visceral and nurturing.

Ways of Heating Sake

In the good old days, we hear, every *izakaya* (page 22) worth its salt had a member of staff with the sole responsibility of warming sake to the perfect temperature. In an ideal world, this is how it would be today: a loving attendant coaxing each flagon of sake to the precise temperature at which its virtues are in full bloom. At the other extreme is the horrid vision of legions of grasping innkeepers chugging sake indiscriminately into the maws of their sake-heating machines; one temperature suits all. The reality, as ever, is somewhere in the middle.

Here are the ways to heat sake. In a restaurant, you are at the mercy of your server. At home, with the discussion of temperature in this chapter, you can experiment with different temperatures until you find the right one for the sake at hand.

Heating sake the proper way: a pewter container filled with sake rests in a bath of hot water.

1 The Sake Machine: *O-kan-ki*. Where these are in use, cleanliness is all important. You will not get your money's worth if remainders sit around in the bottle (or the box) oxidizing for days.

2 The Saucepan. This is the *proper* way to do it. A flask of sake is put in a saucepan of water and slowly brought to the right temperature. If a decanter is placed in a saucepan of freshly boiled water, little bubbles will rise after a couple of minutes. This is the nuru-kan stage; that is, warmed sake. When the bubbles have become a little larger, and immediately start rising to the surface, you have atsu-kan, or hot sake.

3 The Microwave. Japanese microwave ovens often have a button that is pressed when sake is to be heated. Now that's what I call technology. Though admittedly lacking in poetry, this system is tremendously efficient. It is also said that microwaves stir up the alcohol and water molecules, leading to a mellower flavor. If you heat your sake in an open decanter, you will find that the surface is scalding hot, while the rest is still lukewarm. This can be prevented by covering the opening of the decanter.

4 The Kettle. Though I'm sure this system is much frowned upon by purists, it's how we do it at work—so there.

STEP 1: Pour a 1.8-liter bottle of sake into an open kettle.

STEP 2: Rotate the bottle as you pour, creating a whirlpool effect. This gets the sake out of the bottle more quickly and prevents spillage from stop-and-go glugging.

STEP 3: Stick the kettle on the stove and heat as required.

STEP 4: Drink.

5 Self-heating Cups. These little gadgets are attached to a store-bought ration of sake, which they heat automatically when opened. My impression is that you tend to pay more for the container than the sake inside, but the contraption is fabulous nonetheless.

SAKE AND FOOD

Nihonshu wa ryōri wo erabanai

Fine things complement each other. Good food and good drinks are wonderful things and have the captivating ability to combine to produce far more than the sum of their parts. Some combinations work better than others. On the other hand, there are clashes, where two items, gorgeous separately, are gruesome together, in the manner of the death by chocolate that notoriously awaits the wine unfortunate enough to be served with the wrong dessert. There is a feverish note which tends to creep into writing about wine and food; this contrasts with the almost complacent note of confidence in the Japanese saying on the subject: *"Nihonshu wa ryōri wo erabanai."* That is, "Sake doesn't get into fights with food." Sake is very comfortable on the dinner table.

If you are like me, you will find that there are few really unfortunate combinations of food and sake, but, like the "red with meat, white with fish" of wine orthodoxy, a few general guidelines can help make the most of the bill of fare. The balance of sake and food depends first on the volume and persistence of the sake flavor. Go for big, long-finishing sake with strong, richly flavored food, and something light and crisp with a quick finish if you need a selection that won't overpower the taste of delicately flavored food. After "red or white," conversations about wine and food tend to move on to sweet and dry. Sake, too, is often arranged on menus from sweet to dry, indicated with minus and plus signs following numbers as the sake meter value. To my mind, this is a big, fat red herring, and far too limiting. Thinking about a given sake on the axes fruity/crisp/young and earthy/mellow/old will give you a much clearer picture than if you try to understand that sake's complex flavor in terms of only sweet and dry.

Sake is much less acid than wine (good news for tipplers' stomachs), but the level of a sake's acidity is a key point to consider when matching it with food. If you want solid acidity, then the best place to look is well round to the right of the flavor chart—and particularly the junmai and kimoto/yamahai area. Above all, think about how rich your sake is in that full, scrumptious flavor. If it has lots of enveloping rice flavor, it will stand up to strongly flavored food, but its pervasive taste may smother light dishes.

In the following pages are a few observations to start you thinking, or, better still, drinking. Play around and see what works for you, the only person we need to keep happy here. As Slartibartfast said in *The Hitchiker's Guide to the Galaxy* after redesigning the coastline of Africa with fjords, it's far better to be happy than right. I'll start by following the lead of the flavor chart, and considering how different kinds of sake complement different stages of a meal.

Sake Buzzwords
Sake Meter Value •
Nihonshudo

On menus and labels you will often see a number with a plus or minus after it. This is the sake meter value: plus figures indicate dry sake, minus sweet. The higher the figure, the drier (or sweeter) the sake in question. Bear in mind that the flavor on your tongue is strongly influenced by levels of acids and amino acids, so the sake meter value alone does not always reflect precisely how sweet or dry the sake will taste to you.

Choosing the Moment: Before and After

Aperitifs

An opening gambit calls for something light with a crisp finish. Heavy, lingering flavors will spoil the later fun. Low-alcohol sake makes a good starter, if it is not too sweet. In Japan, unfortunately for sake sales, beer has become the almost automatic choice as an opener. If you want to find an alternative to that, carbonated sake might be a good tactic—or you may prefer to think of it as a parallel to a preprandial glass of champagne. Fizz hits the festive spot at the stage of the initial toast, too. The vibrant flavor and aroma of unpasteurized sake is very appetizing, and lightish nama-zake makes a good choice before dinner. Alternatively, you may want to serve very fragrant sake of some kind. Deluxe dai ginjō might sound a rather high-end start to a meal, but the delicate scents will reward the undivided attention, and clean, bitter elements of flavor will prepare the palate for what is to follow.

After-Dinner Drinks

The meal is finished, and the company, relaxed and replete, retires for brandy and liqueurs. What are you, as a sake buff, going to use to settle your guests' stomachs and soothe their souls? Port is a classic postprandial pleasure, and the nearest sake has to that is rich, sweet, sour and complex *kijōshu* (page 50). Otherwise, mature sake is your secret weapon here. Rich *koshu* (page 46) is wonderful for after-dinner sipping, especially sweeter examples. When I introduce unsuspecting Japanese people to old sake, I often tell them to approach it as if it were whiskey or brandy. As a nightcap or fireside snifter, a glass of hoary, mature sake will do the job as well as any single malt.

With the Meal: Sake and Different Cuisines

Japanese Food

The match between Japanese food and sake is so sublime that many sake lovers never look any further. On its home ground, sake is simply unbeatable. Perhaps its most striking attribute is the magical way in which it marries with seafood—especially the uncooked variety.

I think it is easy to be too precious about matching food and drink, but try eating sushi with beer to find out just how grim the wrong combination can be. If you have not already encountered it, this is the quickest way to internalize the Japanese expression *namagusai*. Literally meaning raw stink, it refers to the fishy smell that is greatly amplified by beer, and by many wines.

Although the clash is at its most bloodcurdling with raw fish, the same distressing phenomenon does occur with many cooked or dried seafood dishes, too. With sake, this unpleasant sensation is alchemized into a delicious harmony. An indispensable cooking ingredient in its own right, sake is also a heavenly accompaniment to dishes flavored with soy sauce or *miso*, a salty paste made of fermented soybeans that is vital to Japanese cooking and the Japanese diet. Matched with the subtly flavored foods in which Japanese cuisine abounds, sake complements the delicate tastes and textures so easily swamped in other combinations.

Grilled fish with Japanese pickled ginger. The harmony of sake and fish dishes is a natural.

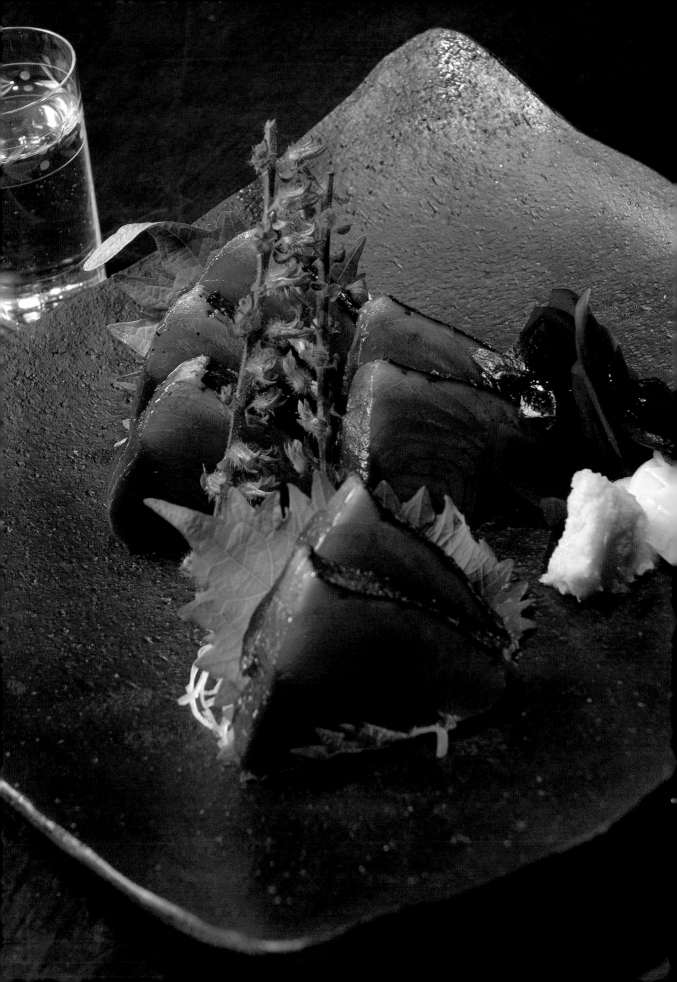

Sushi and Sashimi

Sushi has become a truly international food. For the uninitiated, let me explain that sushi is a variety of sliced toppings (mainly raw seafood), served with rice seasoned with sweetened vinegar. A few of the toppings, like egg, prawn, octopus, and eel, may be cooked first. There are a number of styles of sushi. The best-known kind (with the topping and a dab of *wasabi*—a word translated by humorist Dave Barry as "nuclear horseradish"—on a little fistful of rice) is called *nigiri-zushi*. Other common varieties are *chirashi-zushi,* where the toppings are scattered on a bed of rice, and *maki-zushi*, where the rice and the toppings (if the word applies in this case) are rolled and wrapped in *nori* seaweed.

Sashimi is sushi minus the rice. Most consists of raw fish, crustaceans, and shellfish, although whale, horse, and chicken meat also occasionally feature.

Matching with Sake: I cannot say this too often: sake is a superlative companion to all things fishy. Lighter sake suits the delicate flavors of fresh seafood best. Look on the left of the flavor chart for lighter-bodied brews—airy ginjō, crisp honjōzō, or even a young, springy nama-zake. The lighter-punching range of junmai sake can add to the harmony with its texture, but a full-blooded acidic junmai may overpower those subtle sashimi or sushi flavors. The same is true for the gutsy umami taste of the kimoto/yamahai camp.

Some kinds of shellfish served as sushi toppings have bitter accents that can find a wonderful complement in the bitter flavor elements of sake—not the meaty umami-linked bitterness of aged sake or yamahai, but the fine bitterness of crisp sake found on the left of the flavor chart. The harmony of fresh seafood and sake is not of this world.

酒
の
温
度

Temperature Again

It is always a good idea to think about temperature when drinking sake, and when you are thinking about food matches the same rule applies. If you find the sake is losing the battle with the food, you can draw out its sweetness and body by warming it up a little. However, you do not necessarily have to heat the sake; it will show a quite different side if you just give it half an hour in the bottle out of the fridge—or a few minutes in the glass.

Chikuha, Dai Ginjō

BRAND: Chikuha
TYPE: Dai ginjō
BREWERY: Kazuma Shuzō, in Ishikawa Prefecture

Back in the 1970s, the rise of Ishikawa sake in the National Assessment for New Sake won the prefecture the nickname Ginjō Kingdom. The driving force was the Kanazawa yeast developed by the Kanazawa Regional Taxation Bureau, which is now available nationally as Association Yeast No. 14. Ginjō sake made with this yeast has clean fragrances of fruit like apples and pears, and slender, elegant lines with low acidity. This sweet-smelling example shows a complex of apple and peach scents. The delicate elegance of the fragrance is mirrored in the willowy lines of the flavor. This is sake made to harmonize with the fresh seafood that is the delight of the Hokuriku region.

Tempura: Deep-Fried Whatsits

Another of the Japanese dishes that is widely known overseas, tempura is made from a wide variety of ingredients, mainly vegetables and seafood, deep-fried in batter. Fresher is better with tempura: ideally, you want each portion to go from the hand of the chef to your plate by the shortest possible route. Tempura is usually dipped in a clear broth with piquant flavoring like grated daikon radish or ginger, or eaten with salt or sometimes lemon juice.

Matching with sake: Take a hint from the lemon, and look for something with a solid level of acidity. This will see you playing on the right-hand side of the flavor chart, with a juicy junmai, for example. The higher acidity of yamahai sake also makes a melting accompaniment to the delicate oiliness of good tempura.

◄ Bonito sashimi. Marvel at the heavenly marriage of sake with raw seafood.

Sukiyaki and Other *Nabe* Dishes

Nabe means a pot, and this word is a catchall for any number of dishes with food cooked in a big dish. Places specializing in nabe usually cook them at the table in front of the customer. They can be made with a wide range of ingredients from vegetables to entrails. Best known in the West is sukiyaki, sliced beef cooked with vegetables. Compared to the light flavors of so-called *mizutaki* (water-cooked) nabe specialities like *shabu-shabu*, sukiyaki is quite sweet, richly seasoned with soy sauce, sugar, and/or the sweet, almost-but-not-quite-sake condiment known as *mirin*.

Matching with sake: Pairing this hearty winter warmer with the wallflower flavors of a light dai ginjō (a common choice) would not do the food, the sake, or you any favors. If you insist on ginjō, look for junmai ginjō with plenty of ricey body, or a ginjō that has been aged to give extra umami depth. There is no need to work hard to find a ginjō match, though; a rich-flavored hon-jōzō will work well and show up less on the bill. Something further to the right of the flavor chart will also complement those down-to-earth flavors—sukiyaki will go swimmingly with a hearty junmai, a tangy, complex kimoto-style sake, or even the pungent pleasures of older sake.

Nabe dishes are food to take the chill from the bones in winter, and they are helped delight-fully in this task by warm sake. Piping hot nabe food is perfectly matched to the kinds of sake that work well heated, for a really heart-warming combination.

Tofu

The delicately flavored blocks of soybean curd are one of the group of Japa-nese foods that has become internationally known. As a standard ingredient of miso soup, it is one of the most common items on Japanese tables. Other popular ways of serving it are in nabe dishes, or simply cold *hiya-yakko* with scallions, ginger, or other condiments. The last-suggested serving method is a refreshing standard on the summer tables of Japanese households.

Matching with sake: The fine tofu flavors require delicate sake to comple-ment rather than drown them out. *Yuzu* (Japanese citron), tangy *ponzu* sauce (a light citrus-based sauce), and ginger are common flavorings, and their piquancy is perfectly complemented by the fine body and fragrance of ginjō sake. Lighter sakes in the honjōzō and junmai area may also go well. Fat, umami-rich brews will block out the fine flavors, so look for crisp, light sake that flits across the palate rather than lingering richly. *Yu-dofu* is a finely flavored nabe dish based on tofu, and is great with crisp, clean-edged sake flavor. Unless it is deep-fried, tofu is happiest well on the left of the flavor chart.

Yakitori

Literally meaning grilled chicken, this eponymous dish is chunks of chicken grilled on a skewer. But it is not entirely about chicken, as you will find other meats and vegetables on the menu, too. *Yakitori* restaurants tend to the cheap and cheerful, and are good places for sake hunting. Sadly, sushi places (in Japan, anyway) tend to be so absorbed in the mystique of the food that sake is rather neglected.

Matching with sake: Since few yakitori restaurants limit themselves only to yakitori, their menus are generally diverse enough to offer a match for

A thick soup with crabmeat and tofu. Tofu's subtle flavor cries out for the most delicate of companions.

whatever kind of sake you may feel like drinking. As for yakitori itself, one of the key points is the choice of flavoring. This kind of food is either seasoned with salt, or with a rich, sweet sauce called *tare*. Some restaurants specialize in one or the other, some ask the customer to choose; still others make the decision ingredient by ingredient. The salted version is relatively light in flavor, the tare-flavored style heavier, which means they need different accompaniments to make the best combination. Tare is better with something from the full-bodied right of the flavor chart: salted offerings want something a little lighter, preferably crisp and dry with a smart finish.

Western Food

For many sake drinkers, the combination with Japanese food is so beguiling that they rarely get around to trying it with other styles of cuisine. Yet, despite a widespread Japanese prejudice to the contrary, sake goes well with many non-Japanese dishes. No one has any problems imagining sake with grilled white meat, poached fish, or other, lighter dishes. But I have often heard it said that sake does not go with cream or cheese (dairy products are not part of the traditional Japanese diet). I would agree that it is much simpler to find a red wine that will complement that smelly blue cheese you have bought than to hunt for sake which will stand up to it happily. However, if you stay clear of Gorgonzola and Stilton extremes, pure-rice sake with creamy, cheesy aromatic elements is excellent with dishes using those ingredients. For particularly cheesy things, or cheese

Drinkers' Food

Certain foods are strongly associated with drinking and are often known as *otsumami*. This is an honorific formed from the verb *tsumamu*, to pick something up by the fingertips (or chopsticks). Another expression for food specifically intended as an accompaniment to sake is *sakana* (written with the character 肴—rather than 魚, which is pronounced identically and means fish). Below are a few of the bits and pieces to be found at the elbow of drinkers in Japan—sakana every sake fan should try at least once.

Chinmi Delicacies

At the top of the nibbler's hierarchy are the mysteriously named *chinmi*, written with characters meaning rare and taste, which pretty much conveys the idea. Every possible genre in Japan, from views and gardens to blue cheese and brewers' unions, has its official top-three ranking and these delicacies are no exception. The Three Great Delicacies, as established by the consensus of connoisseurs of the Edo period (1600–1868), are *uni*, *karasumi*, and *konowata*. The first and most common is sea urchin, a popular (although rather expensive) topping for sushi. Karasumi is mullet roe, salted and preserved by drying. It is usually served thinly sliced, and looks unspectacular, but its rich, subtle flavor is superb. It may be served as is, or lightly grilled, in which case the flavor takes on an aromatic, toasty, extra dimension. The third of the great trio is konowata, which is a crunchy variety of *shiokara* (see next entry) prepared from the entrails of the sea slug. Really.

Shiokara: Salt-Pickled Thingummies

Fish, shellfish, and various bits of their insides are the most common ingredients. The various salty bits and pieces come in a range of slime-creature colors and textures. The most common version is the pinkish one made from squid, called *ika no shiokara*. One of the foods traditionally loathed by Western visitors, these delicacies are certainly an acquired taste. I have been told that it is the amino acids, which accumulate in the curing process, that make them go so well with sake.

Tsukemono: Japanese Pickles

A wide variety of ingredients are pickled in a number of bases—salt, rice bran (*nuka*), soy sauce, vinegar, miso, *kōji* (see pages 44 and 85), and the caked lees (*kasu*) left over when sake is pressed. The length of time varies from a few hours for *ichiyazuke* (one-night pickles), to a few months for vegetables done in salt and rice bran (*takuan*, made from the *daikon* radish, is the most popular), and several years for the famous Nara speciality of vegetables (primarily *shirorui*, a relative of the melon) pickled in sake lees. With such a range of flavors—from the light touch of ichiyazuke, to the vinegary tang of purple Kyoto *shibazuke* and the rich years' worth of taste in a slice of *narazuke*—it is easy to find the perfect companion for the lightest of ginjō or the funkiest of koshu.

Japanese pickles: a traditional favorite with sake.

itself, the yoghurty nuances of kimoto or yamahai sake are a perfect complement. Unpasteurized sake is also wonderful with cheese. If you are cooking with butter or cream, a mature sake with a fatter flavor and an oilier texture is just the ticket. For oily dishes, a tart junmai sake with plenty of body and a *shibumi* astringency is ideal. Full-flavored stews are excellent with any sake that works well at room temperature and above.

Both nama-zake and fragrant ginjō styles are relatively new on the scene, and both genres are good places to look for partners to non-Japanese dishes with which more traditional styles are conventionally held to struggle. Fragrant ginjō harmonizes surprisingly with tart-flavored meat dishes. Food cooked with herbs finds a complement in the more fragrant styles of sake, as do vinegar dressings.

Umami is the soul of sake flavor, and tomatoes are one of the richest sources of umami (again, see page 41). Yet that zesty tomato taste tends to put the boot to the gentle flavor of traditional pasteurized styles of sake. It goes much better with the zingy bitter notes of young nama-zake brews, which are great with pizza or pasta.

If you want to keep drinking right through dessert, vintage sake is excellent with sweet Western dishes. The flavor of aged sake often has a solid bitter element, excellent with cakes and tarts, or even over vanilla ice cream.

Chinese Food

In the United Kingdom, some Chinese restaurants have sake on the menu. This seems peculiar from a Japanese standpoint, but makes perfect sense from the point of view of the food. Apart from the lightest sake, most will go happily with a Chinese meal.

Compared to Japanese food, many Chinese dishes have a stronger flavor, and the heavier styles of sake make the best companions. Although more richly flavored junmai ginjō products do well, the rich, earthy rice flavors of pure-rice sake are generally a better match. The complex bitter/astringent profiles of yamahai or kimoto sakes are great with rich, savory dishes, and their acidity combines wonderfully with food cooked in oil, too. Japanese people, when encountering very old sake for the first time, often exclaim "*shōkōshu!*", reminded of the treacly Chinese drink that you can find in almost any Chinese restaurant in Japan. Koshu can make for a pungent harmony when paired with Chinese food.

Spicy Food and Curries

Notwithstanding occasional zingy moments experienced with hot wasabi or the tongue-tingling buzz of *sanshō* (ground seed pods of the Japanese prickly ash), Japanese food is low on spice, and demure traditional sake doesn't get on well with hot food. When I tried matching sake to a variety of Indian curry dishes, I anticipated that a chewy yamahai I had would be the best match. In fact, the winner that evening was a dai ginjō with a firm body and a deep fragrance. Wine people say that the flowery fragrances of Gewurztraminer wine from the Alsace region of France are the best bet with spicy Thai food and curries. It would seem that a fuller-bodied ginjō with a solid fragrance is the sake equivalent.

Korean-style barbecue (*yaki niku* in Japan), where various cuts of meat and vegetables are cooked on iron plates or over charcoal, usually at the customer's table, is found in most parts of Japan. The meat is often flavored with a spicy *tare* sauce before cooking, and is generally dipped in a little dish of something similar before eating. A few years back, a Korean sake producer experienced great success with a sake brewed especially for this kind of food: it was an extremely tart, high-acid sake. A big, fat junmai, or a full-bodied yamahai with plenty of tangy body are the best choices to complement the rich meat and sauces of this cuisine.

Izakaya

Coming down to earth brings us happily to the *aka chōchin*, the "red lanterns," which are sometimes the mark of (and the metaphorical name for) the izakaya, which are to Japanese drinkers what the pub is to the British. They come in all shapes, sizes, and price ranges. Food in izakaya is usually ordered in small portions by the dish, and drinking companions may order dozens of little dishes in the course of an evening. The formal dining order is rarely a concern, yet it is worth bearing in mind that your sashimi won't taste of much if you have eaten some very sweet or spicy dish beforehand. The casual, eclectic style of izakaya is a great, relaxed environment to enjoy the versatility of sake with food.

▶ Beef in a Madeira wine sauce. Richly flavored western dishes work best with full-flavored sake— though highly fragrant ginjō sake can chime with zesty meat dishes.

SAKE TASTING

Sake *drinking* is about pleasure and nothing else; sake *tasting* is an attempt to gather as much information about the sake under consideration as possible. Tasters approach the subject primarily with the three senses of sight, smell, and taste (perhaps with a little tactile input on the palate, too). The basic principles of this exercise can help you squeeze even more hedonistic pleasure from your favorites.

Tasting Equipment and Environment

Sake tasting in Japan has traditionally been done using a special tasting cup (*kiki choko*). Made of white ceramic, it has blue concentric circles painted on the inside. The contrast between the deep blue and the white highlights the clarity (or otherwise) of the sake. When the color is not to be taken into account, cups made of amber-colored glass are used instead. Spittoons are provided so that participants can avoid getting roaring drunk, which can hamper tasting.

Two dark blue rings in the professional taster's sake cup allow drinker's to judge the clarity of a brew.

The tasting room should ideally have plenty of natural light, and the sake should be kept at around 70° F (20° C), which is the temperature that is least forgiving of flaws. The presence of strong odors are a disaster for tasters, so perfume, cologne, and cigarettes are discouraged.

Some restaurants offer tasting sets of several sakes.

Tasting, Stage One—Appearance

Clarity and Impurities

After making sure that there are no alien bodies in the sake, which is extremely unlikely, the next step is to look at the clarity of the brew. If it is cloudy or milky, there are two possible reasons. One reason could be that the sake, one of the group that is made to be cloudy, intentionally contains some sediment (*nigori-zake* or *ori-zake*, page 47), in which case this is not a problem. However, if the sample in question was not made in the nigori style, then there is a problem with the sake. Nowadays, this is an extremely rare occurrence.

粘
性

Legs

Wine types and whiskey people look at the "legs" for clues to the consistency of the sample. The term legs refers to the thickness of the coating left on the side of a glass after wine has been swirled. The use of white porcelain tasting cups for conventional sake tasting means that legs are not easily visible, but by using a glass instead, you can see that there is plenty to be learned about sake in the same way. Young sake is relatively light and fluid, where older sake becomes increasingly viscous. This means that an older sake clings more to the surface of the glass—and that translates to a richer, perhaps even oily, texture on the palate. Pure-rice brews are more viscous than alcohol-added sake, and sweet sake clings to the glass more than dry.

So, having found your sake to be sediment-free (unless it is nigori), it is time to look again at its clarity. I believe the clarity of good sake, more than just the absence of cloudiness, is a positive attribute: a profound transparency seems to sparkle.

AN ESOTERIC NOTE: Sake that has been aged for a long time (five years or more) may contain some sediment, but it is not milky with a sediment like that found in nigori-type products. Depending on the kind of sake and its age, the sediment may produce a translucent cloud or be a muddy sludge. But, since it is almost always filtered out before sale, your chances of encountering it are much, much slimmer than those of your finding sediment in wine.

Color

The natural color of sake at birth, so to speak, is a pale yellow with a slight greenish cast. The depth of color decreases the more the rice is polished, and young dai ginjō sake made from highly polished white rice is almost colorless. The color deepens as sake ages, taking on straw and gold hues, before turning copper, tawny, and darker brown as it moves into the multiyear koshu zone. (A few products made using ancient methods are very dark from the moment they are pressed.) In the case of most types of sake, if one looks down into a tank holding thousands of liters of a brew, one will see that its color is striking, although at the glass-by-glass level, the difference is subtle.

▲ Sake color. At the left is a young orthodox sake, translucent but showing only the palest hint of yellowish color (which can escape the photographer's lens). Next is Kirin's aged ginjō (page 46), with encroaching straw color. Hanahato's Kijōshu (page 50) is dark amber. Kikusakari's Asamurasaki (page 51) is made with an antique red rice strain, lending its pinkish coloring to the sake.

Tasting, Stage Two — Aroma and Flavor

Although we talk of *tasting*, most of what we think of as taste is related to the sense of smell. This is the reason that food seems to lack flavor when one has a blocked nose, and why brewers are very careful not to catch cold: a master brewer (*tōji*) with the sniffles just cannot do his job. Some substances are more volatile than others, which means they escape from the liquid more readily and are smelled more easily. For this reason, the fragrance of sake is taken into account at various stages of brewing.

The Flavor Chart

As a map to help you on your sake journey, I have introduced the Sake Flavor Chart, developed by Haruo Matsuzaki. The chart arranges sake into groups by flavor, starting with the light type at the left, and progressing via mellow and full-bodied to aged at the right. The progression from lighter to fuller flavors and from younger to older sake is an apparently simple story concealing a number of dramas that make a sake drinker's life so much fun. It reflects the fluid, fuzzy reality of sake.

Aperitif	With the meal			With or after the meal			After dinner		
LIGHT	FRESH	FRUITY	DRY	SOFT	MELLOW	SWEET	FULL BODIED	RICH	AGED
Chilled				Cold to warm			Room temparature and above		

"Top Smell"

Judges first sniff the head space of the glass or cup. This "top smell" is known as *uwadachi-ka* in Japanese, which literally means the aroma that rises. The most volatile substances fly off the surface of the sake of their own accord. This process can be helped along by swirling the sake in the cup, just as wine tasters do. At the National Assessment for New Sake, judges look for a good showing of the fruity ginjō aroma—widely considered an indispensable feature of a contender for a gold prize—and for peculiar or unpleasant smells indicating defects. For us pleasure seekers, it is a chance to enjoy the elements of the sake's aroma, which will also, with a little experience, give you a good idea of what kind of flavor to expect.

After the initial sniff to assess the top smell, the taster takes a sip and rolls it around the tongue. This is the stage at which there is a great deal of unsavory slurping, because from now on, the taster simultaneously thinks about taste and smell.

Slurping, Spitting, and *Nodogoshi*

In polite society, both of these actions are frowned upon, yet they are inevitable features of sake tastings. The slurping is done to free up all the aromas for assessment by warming and mixing the fluid with air, and to get the whole of the tongue involved. Spitting is to keep the tasters sober enough to keep working. However, spit as you may, you will still not be sober after several hours of tasting, because the alcohol is absorbed into the bloodstream little by little. (It is a peculiar and regrettable fact that the inebriation that results in these situations has nothing of the "merry" quality that is one of the attractions of social drinking.) If there are only a few sake samples, it is better not to spit out the brew, since you can then assess the way it goes down. This is what the Japanese call *nodogoshi*, and it is an important feature of sake in the real world outside the tasting room.

"Flavor-in-the-Mouth"

Slurping allows air to be mixed with the sake and warmed it on the tongue, so that even more aromatics can be freed. Before and after a sample is spat out, the taster breathes out through the nose in order to consider the new range of scents thus released. These are called *kōchū-ka* (literally, aroma in the mouth) or *fukumi-ka*. (In this case, the verb *fukumu* means to take into the mouth; *ka* means aroma or fragrance.) Aromas that linger on after that are called *modori-ka*.

Taste and Aftertaste

The taster assesses the flavor while rolling the sake around on the tongue. The sake is slurped and swooshed to make sure the whole tongue is covered to give the maximum possible information about taste and texture. Good sake has a balanced flavor—and a good balance of flavors. Bitterness and astringency are no fun if they swamp other tastes, but they are necessary elements of flavor balance. The balance of acidity is also a key factor. That soft, rich satisfying umami flavor is another vital part of the balanced sake mix, and a main component of body. After spitting, the aftertaste will be considered. Some sakes finish in a crisp, quick instant; others linger on with long, persistent flavors.

DRINKER'S PARAPHERNALIA

With Japanese food, the tableware on which the food is served is intrinsic to the overall experience. The colors of the ceramics (white, blue, red, green, black, brown, and any number of combinations and textures) complement the visual pleasure and flavors of the meal. The same is true for *tokkuri*, the thin-necked flasks in which the liquid is served, and sake cups. Each comes in a variety of shapes and sizes and can be acquired for the equivalent of a few dollars, or hundreds, sometimes thousands of dollars. Both top-flight artists and artisans turn out designs. Craftspeople working in ceramics, lacquer ware, bamboo, glass, and wood release works that are eagerly consumed by a discriminating public.

Simple *tokkuri* decanters, elegant and eminently practical for warming sake—form and function perfectly combined.

Sake Cups

Sake cups are called *guinomi, sakazuki,* or *choko* (this last is commonly used in the honorific form, *o-choko*). Choko and sakazuki refer to small cups, guinomi to larger chugging cups. Very tiny cups seem impractical unless you realize they are part of the congenial ritual of *o-shaku*—pouring for one's drinking companion. They are small precisely so that you get to pour more often.

The small size of many sake cups means that there is little head space to swirl the liquid in wine-tasters' fashion. If you want to swirl, a tulip-shaped glass will emphasize the fragrance of that fruity ginjō you bought. For earthier styles, a flatter, oval-shaped glass is better. Specialist wine glasses designed to enhance the characteristics of specific grape varieties can have a startling effect on the quieter sake aromatics. However, should you switch to wine glasses, remember that most sake is more potent than wine. Don't fall into the trap of drinking the same amount as you would were you drinking wine, just because you are drinking from a wine glass, or you could end up with more than you bargained for.

Sake Tasting for Fun

Professional tasters may charge through dozens or hundreds of samples in one sitting. For play rather than work, four or five kinds are plenty. If you can get hold of a range of sake, it is fun to compare different categories.

One way of approaching a tasting is the "matching" system. Up to half a dozen samples are lined up in two rows. In one row, the identity of each sake is clear; the simplest way to do this is just to display the bottle. In a second row, unmarked samples of the same sake are placed, numbered but unlabeled; you can either wrap the bottle in newspaper, or pour a sample of each sake into a glass or tasting cup. The participants try to match the unmarked samples to their labeled counterparts. Although this sounds like the easiest thing in the world to do, it is an excellent way to discover the challenge that is the apparently simple business of tasting.

Flasks

Tokkuri are the little thin-necked decanters used to hold, heat, and pour sake—the thin neck is designed to retain heat. Most hold one or two *gō,* one-tenth or two-tenths of a large bottle of sake, respectively. Each *gō* is 6 fluid ounces (180 milliliters). Ceramic and pewter decanters are used when warming sake, and often come in sets with matching choko. A wide, open-mouthed receptacle called a *katakuchi* is sometimes used to serve sake cold or at room temperature, and these may be made of ceramic or glass. Wooden tokkuri impart a light scent of wood to the sake.

Materials

Ceramics

The history of Japanese ceramics goes back over twelve thousand years. The many schools of Japanese pottery arose as expressions of geology (the clay of a particular region) and local culture—from the poignant simplicity of pots from Tanba, which were originally everyday receptacles made by the area's farmers, to the refinement of Raku ware, inextricably bound to the high culture of the tea ceremony. The sorcerous metamorphosis of the raw materials into expressions as various as shell-like porcelain and the earthy, ashy wonders of the wood-fired Bizen or Shigaraki ceramic ware is an intriguing parallel to the range of transformations that Japan's brewers conjure with rice. The nursery that resulted in such glorious variety in ceramics is the same that nurtured sake, so that drinking sake from Japanese ceramics has a reinforcing effect, amplifying the pleasure of the experience.

There are few activities as pleasant as deciding which sake to drink; choosing the cup is one of them. I find that a crystalline dai ginjō calls out for a delicate cup, and earthy, ricey sake is best sipped from a guinomi with plenty of what potters call *tsuchi-aji*, or an earthy feel. A thick, round-lipped cup delivers the liquid to your palate in a way that is different from that of a wafer-thin edge, and the difference affects the way a sake tastes.

Wood

The humble *masu*, a square box made of *sugi* (Japanese cedar), is one of the most familiar of sake-related images. Sake commonly used to be served in a masu, but its use nowadays is restricted mainly to high days and holidays—festivals and weddings in particular. The masu used at such events are new, and the powerful scent of the wood may overshadow that of the sake itself. Drink from the corner to avoid embarrassing dribbles.

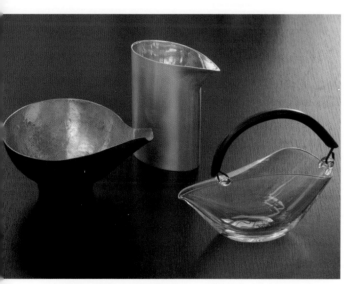

Katakuchi. These open-mouthed decanters come in a wide range of shapes, and are a lovely, elegant way to serve sake. Also excellent for giving sake some air, or gently warming up sake that is overchilled.

Many izakaya drinking establishments serve sake in glasses placed inside masu. This catches any spills, and allows the owner to please favored regular customers by overfilling the glass so that the extra sake is caught in the masu.

You may come across wooden choko or guinomi, for which the most commonly used wood is Japanese cedar.

Lacquer

When visitors from the West discovered the elegant, lustrous products of the perilous craft of coating wood with multiple coats of the poisonous sap of the *urushi* (lacquer) tree, they called it japanning. You may have seen victorious sumo wrestlers drinking from enormous sake cups, closer in dimension to washbasins than toothbrush mugs. These great lacquer receptacles, holding from a measly five *gō* (30 fluid ounces /900 milliliters) to three *shō* (5.7 quarts/5.4 liters), became popular in the Kamakura period (1185–1333). The warrior elite of the time passed these around at drinking parties dignified with the grand name of *sakazukigoto*. However, since to pass a pottery cup of this size around a group of increasingly inebriated warlords would be asking for trouble because of the cup's weight, feather-light, lacquer-ware cups were chosen, although they are delicate in their own way and require careful storage.

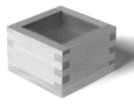

The humble *masu*, once an everyday drinker's tool, is now seen mainly on festive occasions.

Glass and Metal

Pewter tankards and pottery steins aside, it is fairly unusual in the West to drink alcohol from anything but glass. Yet, in Japan, glass vessels for drinking are a newfangled idea, having made their appearance in the nineteenth century, and having gained real popularity still more recently. Although wine glasses are sometimes used, it is more fun to use glass choko, which come in all shapes and sizes. Cold sake is great in glass cups.

Sake cups made of metal (mainly pewter) do exist, but are rather rare.

SAKE LABELS

The shelves of a sake shop are a captivating place to browse: Sake packaging is simply beautiful. Domestic Japanese labels can be a triumph of form over function as far as English speakers are concerned, but if you are aware of the few mandatory items of information listed below, you can soon find out what you need to know without the necessity for Japanese classes.

Obligatory Items for Sake Labels

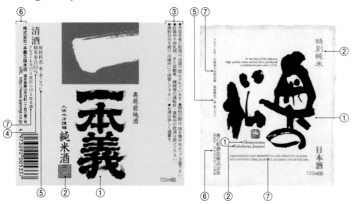

① Name (grade) of product
② Type of sake
③ Warning message: Sake is for those over 20 (酒は20才になってから)
④ Rice-polishing ratio (精米歩合)
⑤ Ingredients (原材料)
⑥ Name and address of brewery
⑦ Percentage of alcohol (アルコール度数)
⑧ Date of production (製造年月日; indicates shipping date)

Although the above are the only items the manufacturer is required to display, many voluntarily give more information, such as the sake meter value, the variety of rice used, and the recommended serving temperature. Some producers even offer a long list of brewing specifications. The example given here provides as much information of this kind as you are ever likely to find.

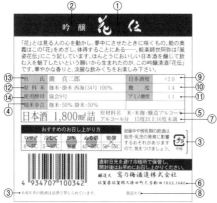

⑨ Sake meter value　日本酒度
⑩ Acidity　酸度
⑪ Amino acids　アミノ酸度
⑫ Rice variety　原料米
⑬ Name of master brewer　杜氏名
⑭ Yeast variety　使用酵母

chapter TWO

Sake for All Seasons
Types and Styles

Viewing the autumn moon
is a traditional pastime
known as *tsukimi*—and, of
course, it is best done with
a favorite sake in hand.
Naturally, Japanese has a
word—*tsukimi-zake*—for
this sake.

WHAT'S YOUR POISON?

There is sweet sake and dry sake, old sake and young sake, pasteurized and unpasteurized sake. We can keep adding to the list: cheap and expensive; flowery and earthy; warm and cold. Every time you buy a glass or a bottle of sake, you have to forge through a forest of possibilities. In the following pages, I introduce the different kinds of sake and their characteristics to help you find the shortest route to the sake that will give you the most pleasure. To put some meat on the theoretical bones, the inimitable sake journalist Haruo Matsuzaki has kindly selected and reviewed a cellar-full of fine sakes, and provided some insights into their creators, especially for this book.

So, down to the nitty-gritty. While we're about it, we may as well start with the bee's knees and the cat's pajamas—the elite Premium group at the top of the pricing pile.

Boiled soybeans, lightly salted. *Edamame* are a classic drinker's nibble.

Yamada Nishiki brewers' rice. From the bottom: unpolished brown rice (100 percent), followed by rice polished to 90 percent of its original size (roughly equivalent to ordinary white table rice), 70 percent (for junmai and honjōzō sakes), 50 percent (for ginjō sake), and 35 percent (for dai ginjō). Note the opaque white center, the mark of a true brewers' rice.

PREMIUM SAKE

Sake is made from rice—not brown rice, but white rice, from which the outer portion has been milled (or polished). The degree of polish is the single most important element determining the grade, flavor, and price of sake, and a defining element of Premium Sake. (In this book, the term Premium Sake is equivalent to the Japanese *tokutei meishōshu*, which translates literally as special designation sake.) Although Premium Sake still accounts for only about one-quarter of all sake made in Japan, it is highly likely it will become your playground.

Junmaishu • Pure-Rice Sake

Rice and water are the elemental building blocks of sake, and that made with nothing else is called *junmaishu, or junmai*. Even before the bottle is opened, its image as the essential, pure form of sake strikes a psychological cord with many drinkers.

If you are looking for full flavor and lots of character, this is a fertile (to say nothing of earthy) furrow for you to plough. This kind of sake is rich in flavor elements (tannin-like astringency, bitterness) that don't sound like a good idea by themselves, but are fantastic in the matrix of elements that make up the splendid liquid in your glass.

You get more of everything with junmai. More acidity—sour, tangy flavors—more body, and more amino acids than in most other alcoholic drinks; hence its satisfying richness of flavor. Junmai has a deeper color and darkens more quickly during aging than other types of sake, a visual (and, in fact, chemical) reflection of the stronger flavors. The one thing you get less of than with other types of sake is a fragrant, floral bouquet. You may come across the odd floral example, but most brewers aim for an earthier (not to mention ricier) style in this category. The aromas and flavors of the rice are at their clearest and most prominent in this type, although butter and cream, and even cheesy aromatic elements, are also common.

In the original 1990 guidelines for Premium Sake, all sakes in this elite group had to be made from rice polished to 70 percent or less of its original size. This meant that an 80-percent sake like Izumibashi's junmaishu, introduced on the next page, could not be labeled thus. When a big maker started selling a low-polish product just like this, calling it "rice-only sake," it created so much confusion that the restriction on the grade of white rice for pure-rice sake was removed in 2004. Now, most brands in the junmai category are still made from rice polished to less than 70 percent of its original size, but there are exceptions.

Tokubetsu Junmai • Special Junmai

This "special junmai" must be made with rice polished to 60 percent or less of its original size, or made using special methods (specified on the label). The higher polish of the rice tends to mean lighter, less earthy flavors, but there is too much overlap with regular junmai to make it worth worrying much about the difference. The only thing to say for certain is that this sake will cost a bit more than the regular junmai from the same brewery.

BUYING SAKE: Sake breweries often have a surprising range of products. Commonly, the various products of a particular firm show both a main brand name and a specific product name. This last may be generic, like *Junmaishu* or *Dai Ginjō*, or be a free-standing original (like the *Umashine* sake made by Ama no To, the alphabetical leader in the Sake Specs chart at the back of the book).

The main brand name is often the name of the company—so the firm that makes Ume no Yado sake is Ume no Yado Shūzo. Sake drinkers tend to think about breweries with their main brand names: few will have heard of the firm Ishimoto Shūzo, but everyone knows about the sake Koshi no Kanbai.

Often, brand and product names are intermingled, or the brand name becomes part of the product name, either by intention or accidentally. To further complicate matters, there is frequent disagreement among retailers as to where the product name stops and the brand name begins. But because the application of product and brand names is far from unified in the sake community, and because sake might also be shelved by brand or brewery, it is best to arm yourself with the product, brand, and brewery names when going shopping.

Oku no Matsu, Tokubetsu Junmaishu

Ama no To, Umashine

Izumibashi, Tokubetsu Junmaishu

Aperitif	With the meal		With or after the meal		After dinner

LIGHT	FRESH	FRUITY	DRY	SOFT	MELLOW	SWEET	FULL BODIED	RICH	AGED

Chilled		Cold to warm		Room temparature and above

SAKE REVIEWS *JUNMAISHU*

Ama no To, Umashine

BRAND: Ama no To (also Heaven's Door)
TYPE: Junmaishu
BREWERY: Asamai Shuzō, in Akita Prefecture

With solid, chunky acidity as a foundation, the combination of bitter, sweet, and astringent elements derived from the rice represent classic junmai. In top form over a wide temperature range, this can be enjoyed chilled or warm. An unfiltered, unpasteurized *genshu* (undiluted sake, with an alcohol level of up to 20 percent; see page 44) version is released with the same label as a seasonal limited edition. The brewery insists on local rice, and *Umashine* conveys a sense of that philosophy.

Oku no Matsu, Tokubetsu Junmaishu

BRAND: Oku no Matsu
TYPE: Tokubetsu junmai
BREWERY: Oku no Matsu Shuzō, in Fukushima Prefecture

The signature impression common to all Oku no Matsu sake is a light, fluent clarity of flavor. Combining the original down-to-earth elements of rice flavor with a sophisticated touch, this particular product is an excellent example of contemporary junmai style.

Izumibashi, Tokubetsu Junmaishu

BRAND: Izumibashi
TYPE: Tokubetsu junmai
BREWERY: Izumibashi Shuzō, in Kanagawa Prefecture

This sake, made from rice that has only been polished to 80 percent, is distinguished by its rough-hewn taste. It has a powerful acidity, and bursts with wild flavor.

Honjōzō • "True Brew Sake"

Honjōzō sake is often made with the loyal regular drinker in mind, and the style is shared by many excellent conservative brews with unobtrusive but invidiously satisfying flavor profiles. Written with characters meaning authentically brewed, honjōzō sake is made with the addition of neutral brewers' alcohol (see "Alcohol-Added Sake" on page 51) to its pure-rice base. Well-made specimens have a smooth texture, usually without the complex grainy feel on the palate of some pure-rice brews. A crisp, clean finish is a frequent attraction. Many brewers choose to work in this style when the key word is dry. The ricey elements tend to be more restrained, often with more neutral aromatics, and a mineral-like feel. The spread of new yeast varieties has encouraged more brewers to make highly scented honjōzō sake, but the tendency in this category is to aim for a quiet, smooth, drinkable profile: lighter-bodied than junmai, and ideal for relaxed, long-haul drinking. Honjōzō products must be made with rice polished to 70 percent or less of its original size.

Tokubetsu Honjōzō

This means special honjōzō. Just as for tokubetsu junmaishu, sake labeled like this must be made from more highly polished rice, or made with special methods, tending toward a lighter flavor. As for the "special" version of this pure-rice sake, the overlap between honjōzō and tokubetsu honjōzō methods from brewery to brewery is too extensive to make this designation helpful, except when comparing different products from the same brewery.

Suehiro, Honjōzō Kira

Koshi no Kanbai, Bessen, Tokubetsu Honjōzō

Aperitif		With the meal			With or after the meal			After dinner
LIGHT	FRESH	FRUITY	DRY	SOFT	MELLOW	SWEET	FULL BODIED	RICH	AGED

Chilled | Cold to warm | Room temparature and above

SAKE REVIEWS HONJŌZŌ

Suehiro, Honjōzō Kira

BRAND: Suehiro
TYPE: Honjōzō
BREWERY: Suehiro Shuzō, in Fukushima Prefecture

Kira is a crisp, extremely dry honjōzō sake with a razor-sharp finish, and the name's similarity to the word "killer" in English has helped make it a popular sake in the United States.

Koshi no Kanbai, Bessen, Tokubetsu Honjōzō

BRAND: Koshi no Kanbai
TYPE: Tokubetsu Honjōzō
BREWERY: Ishimoto Shuzō, in Niigata Prefecture

Light on the palate as it is, *Bessen* gives the impression of an intricately crafted flavor, based on the abundant use of brewers' rice Gohyakuman-goku (see page 83). Although often served chilled by bars and such, this sake shows still richer flavor when warmed.

Ginjō and *Junmai Ginjō* • "Special Brew Sake"

The hallmark of this genre is the marvelous fruity scents conjured from humble grains of rice. To qualify for this tag, sake must be made from rice polished down to 60 percent or less (50 percent or less for dai ginjō, discussed on page 40). The high polish results in the refinement of flavor and higher costs that are the swings and merry-go-rounds in the ginjō playground.

This category has generated its own vocabulary, starting with the generic fragrance, *ginjō-ka* (*ka* meaning a scent or aroma). Signature fragrances come in a wide range of fruity identities— apple, melon, pear, the odd dash of strawberry or citrus, banana, persimmon, lychee, pineapple. Sometimes a single note stands out, but thought-provok-ing fusions are common. Mixed in with all this fruit, you may find flowery, spicy, and estery elements, and notes of anise or licorice as well. These perfumed, volatile elements often overlay more sedate, rice-related flavors and aromas.

The wide range of styles in this category is often thought of in terms of two extremes—one emphasizing the aroma (*kaori ginjō*), and one in which the key is finesse of flavor (*aji ginjō*). There are rice-only ginjō products (junmai ginjō), and alcohol-added ones. Brewers aiming for light body and prominent fragrance tend to take advantage of the technique of alcohol addition; those looking for more depth and soft, rich rice flavor will not.

The method of brewing is known as *ginjō-zukuri* (from *tsukuri*, meaning making). The main characteristic is low-temperature fermentation, giving a lighter, delicate flavor. Balance and elegance of structure are the joy of all good sake; ginjō fans expect their pricier favorites to reward them with that much more poise and class.

Ginjō Versus *Junmai Ginjō*

At this point, I should probably explain why I have rushed in where angels fear to tread by lumping in alcohol-added and pure-rice ginjō together. There is a clear difference between the two at the production stage—the addition of brewers' alcohol, or its omission. Just as for honjōzō and junmai sake, the pure-rice type will leave you with a beefier brew with higher levels of acids and amino acids. Adding brewers' alcohol produces a lighter blend.

However, honjōzō and junmai sakes tend to be brewed with different goals in mind, reinforc-ing the distinctions arising from the differences in production. Most brewers of junmaishu aim for a full-flavored sake, and makers of honjōzō favor bouquet. Moving up to ginjō class and above, however, we find that the generic ginjō bouquet looms much larger in the minds of brew-ers and consumers alike. The trend is for the brewer aiming to make a particularly fragrant sake to add alcohol to retain the aromatic elements, whereas those wishing to emphasize flavor will work in the pure-rice style. People talk about kaori ginjō and aji ginjō to describe these two poles of ginjō style. Still, distinguishing stylistically between ginjō sake with and without alcohol addi-tions is tricky. And further, a ginjō (or junmai ginjō; the term ginjō indicates both from now on) with none of the fruity, flowery fragrances for which the genre is famous will find few admirers.

Ōka Ginjōshu

Aperitif	With the meal				With or after the meal			After dinner	
LIGHT	FRESH	FRUITY	DRY	SOFT	MELLOW	SWEET	FULL BODIED	RICH	AGED

Chilled   Cold to warm   Room temparature and above

Urakasumi Zen   *Kaden Ginjōshu*

Kokuryū, Junmai Ginjō

SAKE REVIEWS | GINJŌ AND JUNMAI GINJŌ

Kaden Ginjōshu

BRAND: Mado no Ume
TYPE: Ginjō
BREWERY: Mado no Ume Shuzō, in Saga Prefecture

With bitter and tangy elements as an undercurrent, and an excellent crisp finish to restrained and complex flavors, this ginjō makes a superb example of the aji-ginjō type—the emphasis being on flavor rather than aroma.

All this brewery's products share a stylish visual presentation, giving an impression of elegance in harmony with the quality of the sake itself.

Ōka Ginjōshu

BRAND: Dewazakura
TYPE: Ginjō
BREWERY: Dewazakura Shuzō, in Yamagata Prefecture

It is no exaggeration to say that this is the brand that made the expression ginjō generally familiar. *Ōka*, meaning cherry blossom, is a standard wherever sake is sold. The flamboyant aromatics and light, smooth texture, redolent of the bewitching blossoms of the cherry tree, delight its many fans in Japan and, recently, overseas—especially in the United States.

Kokuryū, Junmai Ginjō

BRAND: Kokuryū
TYPE: Junmai ginjō
BREWERY: Kokuryū Shuzō, in Fukui Prefecture

With refreshing apple- and grape-like aromatics wafting through taut, crisp texture on the palate, *Kokuryū Junmai Ginjō* has a feeling of transparency, hinting at its origins along the chilly Japan Sea coast. It makes a great complement to dishes made with fresh seafood.

Urakasumi Zen

BRAND: Urakasumi
TYPE: Junmai ginjō
BREWERY: Saura, in Miyagi Prefecture

Made from the local table-rice variety, Toyo Nishiki, the *Zen* label (yes, *that* Zen) has a proud record of more than four decades of sales. With its subdued aromatics, this sake is excellent for relaxed drinking during dinner, and is distinguished by a smooth texture that never cloys.

Dai Ginjō and *Junmai Dai Ginjō* • The Ultimate Special Brew

So we reach the apex of the sake pyramid. Whether *dai ginjō* is the apotheosis of the sake experience for you will depend on your personal preferences: what is certain is that it will cost you more to buy, just as it cost the brewer more to make. At this level, the brewer aims for delicate sophistication of flavor, and elegant aromatics to match. Levels of acids and amino acids are lower still, and you can expect all the flavor characteristics listed for the ginjō category, but generally stronger fragrance and lighter body. Rice-related taste and aromatics are whittled down to a clean, crisp, finely honed point to give the flavor a strong sense of transparency.

Flowery, spicy and, above all, fruity fragrances take center stage. You can find a detailed discussion of serving temperatures elsewhere in this book, but this is a good moment to point out that the more florally fragrant styles of sake require chilling to show their best.

There are dai ginjō products made by machine, but they are the exception. Hand-brewing is the rule. The master brewer will have used every loving, laborious, trick in his book. Costly brewer's rice polished to less than half of its original size, and carefully selected ginjō yeast (many strains of which are notoriously temperamental) are also key elements in the making of this highest grade of sake. The *basic* requirement is rice polished to 50 percent or less, but 40 percent or less is not uncommon with luxury brands. Sake made for entry in the national annual trade contest is routinely made from rice that has been polished to 35 percent of its original size, tiny pearls from the heart of the grain.

Until recently, ginjō sake was made exclusively for entry in trade contests, and was unknown to the ordinary consumer. The very word ginjō has only become a part of the average drinker's vocabulary in the last couple of decades. Although ginjō (including dai ginjō) production accounts for only 7 percent of all sake produced, its spread has influenced theory and practice throughout the industry. As for the customers, even people who rarely drink sake now know ginjō as a synonym for quality and style. Since the sake industry talks of its history in terms of centuries, ginjō remains a recent arrival. Nonetheless, the charisma of the genre has become one of the industry's most potent weapons.

| Ōnakaya, Junmai Dai Ginjō |
| Rikyūbai, Junmai Dai Ginjō |
| Biwa no Chōju, Dai Ginjō |

Aperitif	With the meal	With or after the meal	After dinner
LIGHT	FRESH	FRUITY	DRY	SOFT	MELLOW	SWEET	FULL BODIED	RICH	AGED
Chilled	Cold to warm	Room temparature and above

Masuizumi, Junmai Dai Ginjō

Junmai Dai Ginjō, Sanka

SAKE REVIEWS *DAI GINJŌ AND JUNMAI DAI GINJŌ*

Biwa no Chōju, Dai Ginjō

BRAND: Biwa no Chōju
TYPE: Dai ginjō
BREWERY: Ikemoto Shuzō, in Shiga Prefecture

This brewery excels at big-boned sake, rich in sweetness and tangy acidity. With the density of flavor from Yamada Nishiki rice as a keynote, the compelling quality of this sake is enveloped in a gorgeous fragrance. This makes it a model of one contemporary style of dai ginjō, with its powerful impact in terms of both fragrance and flavor.

Masuizumi, Junmai Dai Ginjō

BRAND: Masuizumi
TYPE: Junmai dai ginjō
BREWERY: Masuda Shuzō-ten, in Toyama Prefecture

The clean top aromatics are like apples, concealing rounded flavors that harmonize beautifully. Acidity brings focus to the whole by delineating the edges, without ever being intrusive.

Ōnakaya, Junmai Dai Ginjō

BRAND: Shichiken
TYPE: Junmai dai ginjō
BREWERY: Yamanashi Meijō, in Yamanashi Prefecture

Yeast No. 1601, with which this brand is brewed, only recently made its big entry with a flourish of remarkably dynamic aromatics. This sake gives a powerful first impression of ripe fruit leading into a light, uncluttered flow of flavor. A good, harmonious combination of strong fragrance and light flavor.

Rikyūbai, Junmai Dai Ginjō

BRAND: Rikyūbai (also Tōzai, Mukune, Root of Innocence)
TYPE: Junmai dai ginjō
BREWERY: Daimon Shuzō, in Osaka Prefecture

From refreshing strawberry-like top notes, a crisp touch on the tongue is followed by a youthful acidity that positively bounds around the mouth. The fresh quality of the sake gives a first impression of bold, crisp lines, but there is also a definite contribution from a densely compacted umami-rich rice flavor.

Junmai Dai Ginjō, Sanka

BRAND: Masumi
TYPE: Junmai dai ginjō
BREWERY: Miyasaka Jōzō, in Nagano Prefecture

Miyasaka's *Sanka* has vivid fragrances of peach, banana, and vanilla that rise up and up. Its youthful flavors burst on the palate with a freshening sensation. In a poetic touch, the name that has been given this sake, *Sanka*, is written with the characters for mountain flower.

旨味

Sake Buzzword
Umami

Traditional thinking in Japan about tastes in the West assumed four basic flavors: sweet, sour, salty, and bitter. Nowadays, the Japanese word "umami" has been added to the list. It is the taste found in the "hearty" flavor of tomatoes, cheese, and meat, and as a key element in the flavor of sake. Whether as a noun, or in its adjectival form of *umai*, it is a very tricky word to translate — savory, meaty, and tasty being a few of the attempts to date. The issue is further complicated by the fact that umami also means delicious in a general sense. The best translation I can manage is richness, a satisfying roundness of flavor. That works for sake drinkers, I believe. Umami in sake is often related to amino acids (in which sake is rich), and it is probably not going too far to say that sake people are obsessed with the umami flavor derived from rice.

EXPRESSIONS

Nama-zake: The Live Stuff—Unpasteurized Sake

One of the rising stars of the modern sake world is unpasteurized, or nama, sake, the nama being written with the character 生, meaning alive. *Nama-zake* really is alive—containing living yeast and active enzymes, which means it is prone to spoil and that refrigeration is a must during storage. Once only to be had by the lucky folk who did the brewing, the spread of refrigerated facilities for storing and transport has made this zesty tipple widely available domestically, though it is rarely exported.

Most of the nama-zake you will ever drink will be very young (under a year old), and zip, zing, and freshness are what they provide, and what most of its fans seek. I'm very fond of aged nama-zake, with its rather outré notes, rich with ripe tropical fruit overtones and fat, spicy flavor, but the eccentric tastes and problems of storage mean it is likely to remain on the fringes, if not actually beyond the pale.

Fresh and fruity is the general nama refrain. Look for lively, refreshing tastes, with a boisterous spicy feeling of young green shoots and fresh-cut wood, light nutty flavors, and perhaps a citrus accent. Other fruit scents also make their appearance—but green rather than ripe apples, zesty grapefruit rather than sweet banana. There is often a spicy—even peppery—edge to the fragrance. The sour tang of unpasteurized brews tends to stand out, and a cleansing bitter-astringent note is a common element in nama flavor profiles, too. This sometimes contributes to a quick, clean finish, though the very same sharp, green elements provide a lingering aftertaste in some cases.

SAKE REVIEWS *NAMA*

Dassai, Junmai Ginjō 45 Nama-zake

BRAND: Dassai
TYPE: Nama junmai ginjō
BREWERY: Asahi Shuzō, in Yamaguchi Prefecture

Together with the fragrances of melon and strawberry, this brims with the refreshing flavors typical of unpasteurized sake. Although astringency and acidity are key components of the flavor, it is consistently smooth. The product is on sale only seasonally, from April to October.

Funaguchi Kikusui, Ichiban-shibori, Honjōzō Nama Genshu

BRAND: Kikusui
TYPE: Nama-zake
BREWERY: Kikusui Shuzō, in Niigata Prefecture

With a skillful combination of sweet elements and a high level of alcohol (19 percent), this has the round, fat flavor that is one expression of the nama style. It has a rich, thick flavor overall, with a definite sweetness on the palate. Apart from this standard, an aged version of the sake is also marketed.

Nama Chozōshu • Almost Unpasteurized Sake

Stored unpasteurized, and heated only once before shipping, this could be thought of as a semi-nama-zake. The aim is to retain as much as possible of that fresh nama feel, while avoiding the storage problems.

Junmai Ginjō, Shukon

BRAND: Tama no Hikari
TYPE: Nama chozō junmai ginjō
BREWERY: Tama no Hikari Shuzō, in Kyoto

Tama no Hikari sake is characterized by a thick flavor centered on solid acidity. This solid-bodied, big-boned junmai ginjō is no exception, but the plump, round flavor is augmented in this case by a refreshing impression, typical of the *nama-chozō* style. By giving both strong acidity and powerful flavor full rein, the makers succeed in bringing out an excellent sharp finish.

Kimoto and *Yamahai*

These closely related styles are named for traditional methods of making the yeast starter (more about this on page 87), which yield rich, complex flavored sake. The sheer time and labor involved in these methods means that they were shuffled to the side as less strenuous methods for making sake were developed. Yeast starter made by the modern quick-fermenting method smells like essence of ginjō—fruity and tangy and light. *Yamahai* and *kimoto* offer a more complex, dense, and earthy set of aromas—yogurt and spice, cloves and nuts—and some of these are carried on to the finished sake. When sniffing a batch of yamahai starter, the sharp-nosed are often heard to cry, "Yogurt!" This is neat olfactory shorthand for the scents of lactic acid that are a feature of the style. As it ages, nutty (sometimes even woody) notes emerge.

These venerable techniques produce sake with higher levels of organic and amino acids. To the drinker, this means lots of body and powerful, tangy flavors. (It also means that sake made in this way tends to have a deeper color.) There is more texture to the acidity of this kind of sake. What your yamahai (or kimoto) fan wants is for the beloved tipple to serve up a considerable punch, with solid acidity and plenty of rich, satisfying umami flavor. Kimoto-school sake often has prominent bitter/astringent elements and a grainy feel. These features, rough-edged when the sake is cold, blossom into a rich, round, full flavor when it is warmed.

Aperitif		With the meal			With or after the meal			After dinner	
LIGHT	FRESH	FRUITY	DRY	SOFT	MELLOW	SWEET	FULL BODIED	RICH	AGED
Chilled				Cold to warm			Room temparature and above		

Daishichi, Junmai Kimoto

Daishichi, Junmai Kimoto

BRAND: Daishichi
TYPE: Kimoto junmai
BREWERY: Daishichi Shuzō, in Fukushima Prefecture

This brewer is the most famous practitioner of the traditional kimoto method. Brewing four-fifths of its output in the style, their products are united by a spacious umami concealing a clean sweetness derived from the rice, a characteristic most evident in the junmai ginjō class. In this particular product, the unobtrusively masterful, acidity-based flavor is complemented by traces of ripe-apple fragrance flitting across the palate.

Genshu • Undiluted Sake

The characteristics of *genshu* as a category are all related to the high percentage of alcohol. A combination of the nature of sake yeast and nifty brewing tricks developed in Japan over the centuries means that sake can easily be brewed to a strength of 20 percent alcohol by volume. Most sake is shipped after being diluted to around 15 percent, but some goes on sale undiluted as genshu. (Ginjō brewing has a low yield, giving only about 17 or 18 percent alcohol, so in ginjō you may find genshu in this lower range.) Look for plenty of ethanol-powered punch, with even a fiery feeling on the tongue. Estery and solvent notes are often evident in the nose, and I also tend to pick up a kind of mineral quality (like the smell of slate when it is split). With undiluted sake, there is a sense of all the flavor elements being more intense, giving a dense, often very spicy taste.

| | | | | | *Kasumochi Genshu, Yauemonshu* | | |
| | | | | | *Gokyō, Ginjō Genshu* | | |

Aperitif	With the meal		With or after the meal		After dinner		
LIGHT	FRESH	FRUITY	DRY	SOFT	MELLOW	SWEET	FULL BODIED	RICH	AGED
Chilled			Cold to warm		Room temparature and above		

SAKE REVIEWS *GENSHU*

Gokyō, Ginjō Genshu

BRAND: Gokyō
TYPE: Ginjō genshu
BREWERY: Sakai Shuzō, in Yamaguchi Prefecture

This sake, with its high level of alcohol, has a distinctive crisp aftertaste. This is power ginjō. The contemporary mainstream of ginjō sake is high on fragrance and light in flavor. *Gokyō Ginjō Genshu*, however, is a solid champion of the flavor-driven aji ginjō school.

Kasumochi Genshu, Yauemonshu

BRAND: Yamatogawa (also Yauemon, Tsuki Akari, Rashiku)
TYPE: Genshu
BREWERY: Yamatogawa Shuzō-ten, in Fukushima Prefecture

This intense, sweet sake is made with double the normal amount of *kōji*. The plump sweetness suggests sweet potatoes and chestnuts. The thick texture on the tongue is followed by a surprisingly crisp finish thanks to an adroit acid tang. Excellent with strongly flavored dishes like grilled eel, or even with dessert.

Low-Alcohol Sake • *Tei-arukōru shu*

The flavor balance of orthodox sake products is due partly to the high level of alcohol. In many low-alcohol sakes (from just a notch or so below the standard 15-to-16-percent range, right down to 5 percent or so), this is compensated for by stronger sweet-and-sour elements to the flavor.

Another tactic is carbonation, which is an effective way of beefing up very light flavors. Bubbles are also a key weapon in the armory of those who set out to muscle in on the market for beer, or the popular *chū-hai* cocktail drinks. You may find an aroma

Sake Buzzword
Kōji

Rice *kōji* is a defining element of sake in terms of production, flavor, and aroma — even the legal definition of sake mentions it. The conversion of the starch of the rice into a fermentable (not to mention edible) sugary form using the metabolism of a kōji mold—a living organism—is the crux of sake brewing. The mold is propagated on steamed rice, and produces enzymes that break down starch molecules into sugar as a source of energy for growth. The quality of a wine is essentially decided by the quality of the grapes at harvest. In the sake world, the raw material must undergo a complex, fundamental transformation at the hands of the master brewer, or tōji, meaning his skill is as vital an ingredient of fine sake as fine rice. The style of kōji strongly influences the style of sake. More information about how kôji is made can be found in Chapter 4.

In the natural world, the particular microorganism used in sake making is found growing on ears of rice hung to dry in the fields after harvest. It would seem that, at some point a couple of millennia or so ago, it found its way into the Japanese brewers' equation as part of the unique system that results in sake.

reminiscent of lemonade or other fizzy drinks—even in still products. Makers of low-alcohol sake frequently have an eye on the affluent female customer, and this is reflected in the incidence of tinted (okay, pink) sake, and packaging accented with flowers, ribbons, and so on.

Ichi no Kura, Himezen

Aperitif		With the meal			With or after the meal			After dinner	
LIGHT	FRESH	FRUITY	DRY	SOFT	MELLOW	SWEET	FULL BODIED	RICH	AGED
Chilled				Cold to warm			Room temparature and above		

SAKE REVIEW *LOW-ALCOHOL SAKE*

Ichi no Kura, Himezen

BRAND: Ichi no Kura
TYPE: Low-alcohol sake
BREWERY: Ichi no Kura, in Miyagi Prefecture

Sweet-and-sour flavors suggest Chinese quince, lemons, and acerola. A honey-like sweetness and refreshing acidity ring in the change on the palate between working distinctly and in combination. Drunk well chilled, this makes a fine aperitif to enjoy before many styles of food.

Shinshu and *Shibori-tate* • Sake Nouveau

At around the time in late fall when Beaujolais Nouveau makes its annual appearance on the drinking world's calendar, sake fans are licking their lips at the thought of the first sake of the season—*shinshu*—new sake. Sake straight from the press is rambunctiously lively, with zesty flavors gamboling in all directions. Aromatically, the striking characteristic is the generic *shinshu-bana*—new sake nose, shorthand for a complex of young, green, and unripe aromas. A close relative is *kōji-bana* (kōji nose), a nutty accent held to derive from the sake mold, kōji. Both of these characteristics fade as sake matures. There is a natural tendency to associate freshly pressed sake (*shibori-tate*) with the nama style, but you may also find it pasteurized. Further, you may find some shibori-tate bottled undiluted as genshu (sometimes, direct from the press), or filtered and diluted before sale.

Miyo-zakura Shibori-tate, Tokubetsu Junmai

Aperitif		With the meal			With or after the meal			After dinner	
LIGHT	FRESH	FRUITY	DRY	SOFT	MELLOW	SWEET	FULL BODIED	RICH	AGED
Chilled				Cold to warm			Room temparature and above		

SAKE REVIEW *SHINSHU AND SHIBORI-TATE*

Miyo-zakura Shibori-tate, Tokubetsu Junmai

BRAND: Miyo-zakura
TYPE: Shinshu, tokubetsu junmai
BREWERY: Miyo-zakura Shuzō, in Gifu Prefecture

This product goes on sale in advance of the spring cherry blossom viewing season, and combines rich, full flavor with a fresh aroma that suffuses the palate. The company, a front-runner in the marketing of freshly pressed shibori-tate sake, offers plenty of variety both in terms of sake style and packaging (including canned products).

Koshu and Jukuseishu • Aged Sake

Most sake is made to be drunk young, within a year or two of production, and aged sake only represents a minute—but, I am happy to report, growing—portion of the whole spectrum. Shinshu is new sake; the aged variety is called *koshu*.

Old sake comes in many shades, from pale ginjō-style sake that has been matured at glacial speeds and arctic temperatures, to pungent, funky, deeply colored sake that has been aged at ambient temperature in great vats. Aging is all about depth. The color shifts from the palest yellowy green cast of new sake to russet, copper, caramel, brown, and chocolate—colors that grow progressively deeper with the years. The aroma also gains in depth; in conjunction with the color, it can tell you most of the story. The odor associated with aged sake is called *jukusei-ka*—literally, the fragrance of maturation. (You may also come across the pejorative equivalent, *hine-ka*, which is often colorfully translated as old stink.) Fresh, green aromas are gradually subsumed in deeper, richer, mature scents, many of which will be old friends to those who enjoy sherry. Whiskey drinkers may be reminded of the scents that derive from the oak in which their favorites are matured, although the aromas in question here do not come from wood but emerge from the sake itself. (With the exception of *taru-zake* and a few experiments aged in wine casks, sake is kept either in bottles, or in enamel or stainless steel tanks.)

Those familiar with the tangy damp hay aromas of noble rot wines will also come across old friends. The sappy, green flavors and odors familiar from conventional young sake give way to nuts, smoke, caramel, chocolate, and other toasty elements. These elements tend to come in tandem with bitter flavor notes, often the key to the balance of taste in koshu.

Sake Kegs at Celebrations

Taru-zake (page 51) is prepared at the brewery, bottled, and sold. This is not the same as the sake in kegs that makes its appearance on high days and holidays in Japan. In the latter case, the kegs are filled just before an event. The festive ritual of cracking open the lid of a keg with wooden mallets is called *kagamiwari*. The kegs used are new, which means the sake takes on a strong wood flavor. If the sake is left in the keg too long before serving, the sharp aroma of the wood will become overpowering, especially since the scent from the keg is reinforced by that of the wooden masu boxes in which it is served.

			Kirin Hizōshu					Momotose 1972	
Aperitif	With the meal			With or after the meal				After dinner	
LIGHT	FRESH	FRUITY	DRY	SOFT	MELLOW	SWEET	FULL BODIED	RICH	AGED
Chilled			Cold to warm			Room temparature and above			

SAKE REVIEWS *KOSHU AND JUKUSEISHU*

Kirin Hizōshu

BRAND: Kirin (also Kanbara)
TYPE: Koshu
BREWERY: Kaetsu Shuzō, in Niigata Prefecture

The characteristically delicate flavor of this sake results from maturing ginjō sake slowly over a long period at low temperatures. To the crisp, clean finish which is the trademark of Niigata sake, this adds a soft, graceful settled feel and a subtle touch of umami flavor. The eye-catching blue bottle makes an ideal gift, and is perfect to open on a special occasion. *See also photograph on page 25.*

Momotose 1972

BRAND: Momotose
TYPE: Koshu
BREWERY: Fukumitsuya, in Ishikawa Prefecture

Momotose is the name reserved for this brewery's lineup of aged sake: this particular example has been matured for over thirty years. The lustrous auburn sake is brim-full of caramel-like sweetness. With elements of pine nuts and other nut flavors mixed in, this dense sake has an overwhelming complexity of rich, mature, and mellow flavors.

Nigori-zake and *Ori-zake* • Cloudy Sake

These two kinds of sake contain milky sediment, which settles to the bottom of the bottle during storage. The bottle is usually shaken before serving, so the sake is milky white when drunk. In the case of the less common *ori-zake*, the sediment may be a barely visible frosting on the base of the bottle; some *nigori-zake*, on the other hand, is more than half full of sediment.

The sediment is made up of remnants of rice and kōji, and also contains lots of yeast. The smell and taste of these three constituents define nigori as a type, and mean that it has a powerful flavor compared to its less murky counterparts. All those solids in suspension also lend this kind of sake a distinctive physical texture on the palate. A large proportion of nigori products are on the sweet side, but there is no scientific reason for this.

Although many of these products are pasteurized to stop yeast and enzyme activity, you may, in Japan, come across an *unpasteurized* product containing sediment. In this case, secondary fermentation in the bottle is possible. Some brewers deliberately aim for this. If this kind of product is shaken like a normal nigori, the results range from regrettable to ruinous, as the contents are under pressure because of the fermentation. Where this kind of fireworks is part of the plan, the product is called *kassei seishu*—"active sake." Open with caution.

Nineteen-gallon (seventy-two-liter) sake kegs adorn the brewery entrance to Doi Shuzō-jō, makers of Kaiun sake (page 64).

Nigori-zake owes its milkiness to rice solids that remain in the brew.

SAKE REVIEW *NIGORI-ZAKE AND ORI-ZAKE*

Tsuki no Katsura, Nakakumi Nigori-zake

BRAND: Tsuki no Katsura
TYPE: Nigori-zake
BREWERY: Masuda Tokubei Shōten, in Kyoto Prefecture

This sake brims with a young aroma of green apples, the steadily fizzing carbon dioxide bubbles bursting pleasantly in the mouth. The level of alcohol is rather high at 17 percent, but the invigorating action of the fizz makes for a surprisingly light effect. Astringency and bitterness at just the right level make this a good match for meat dishes.

Unfiltered Sake • *Mu-roka*

Most sake is filtered as a means of adjusting color and flavor and to enhance stability, but unfiltered sake has its followers. At the start of the sake's life, some color, flavor, and aromatic elements are left in that would have been removed by filtration. The gap widens as the sake ages; *mu-roka* sake matures in quite a distinct way compared to its traditionally filtered counterparts—it is earthier, shaggier, and more complex.

Dealers in this kind of sake tend to stress the natural aspects, with emphasis on the image of it being untouched by human hands. This line of thinking leads to the production of sake that is unfiltered, unpasteurized, and undiluted. Such *mu-roka nama genshu* has received considerable attention in consumer magazines in recent years. The fat, sometimes unruly flavors, and the difficulty with which such products are handled makes them a minority concern, but this style shows every sign of having found a steady niche.

SAKE REVIEW *MU-ROKA*

Kamoshibito Kuheiji, Mu-roka Warimizu Nashi

BRAND: Kamoshibito Kuheiji (also Kuheiji, Niné)
TYPE: Unfiltered sake
BREWERY: Banjō Jōzō, in Aichi Prefecture

The refreshing fragrance is redolent of ripe peaches. There is an almost overwhelming sense of fruitiness to this sake, honey-accented sweetness combining with pervasive sour elements. The well-rounded and intricate taste is in perfect unity with the aromatics, and the concentration of the two, so typical of unfiltered sake, offers a dense matrix to enjoy.

NON-PREMIUM SAKE

The discovery of a cheap, easy-to-drink brew even in distant corners of Japan is one of the modest pleasures of travel here. Especially if you can find sake, with a little cup included, in a railway station shop at the beginning of a long journey. Sake that does not qualify for one of the special designations just introduced is often called *regyura-shu*—regular sake—since this class of products was traditionally the bread-and-butter for most companies. Though widely ignored and sometimes vilified by connoisseurs, well-made examples are entirely respectable. Large additions of brewers' alcohol to the pure-rice base are permitted, leaving the original aroma and flavor characteristics relating to rice less pronounced—their absence lending to the aroma, a mineral feeling that is rather chalky, or stony perhaps. When so-called triple sake is in the blend, you may also pick up candy-sweet elements derived from added sugars. Overall, expect less fruit, less rice, and a more neutral, less lively profile than for Premium Sake. In this range, do not expect a subtly layered complex of fragrance and flavor—but there are respectable chugging sakes to be found. Many are made to be drunk warm.

					Seishu Hakkaisan				
Aperitif		With the meal				With or after the meal		After dinner	
LIGHT	FRESH	FRUITY	DRY	SOFT	MELLOW	SWEET	FULL BODIED	RICH	AGED
Chilled				Cold to warm			Room temparature and above		
									Kenbishi
					Takashimizu, Seisen Karakuchi				

SAKE REVIEWS REGULAR SAKE

Kenbishi

BRAND: Kenbishi
TYPE: Regular
BREWERY: Kenbishi Shuzō, in Hyōgo Prefecture

The signature Kenbishi style involves the meticulous production of opulent, deep-flavored sake, making lavish use of brewers' rice. The combination of an abundance of body and a clean finish is superb. It not only performs well warm, but is excellent cold or even over ice. There is also a well-regarded taru-zake version, which is shipped exclusively to izakaya in wooden casks.

Seishu Hakkaisan

BRAND: Hakkaisan
TYPE: Regular
BREWERY: Hakkai Jōzō, in Niigata Prefecture

Where many breweries are concentrating their energies on Premium Sake, this company has chosen rather to dedicate itself to raising the level of regular-grade products. Whilst sticking firmly to the principle of quality by using highly polished rice and low-temperature storage, the company aims for sake with a soft texture and smooth flavor.

Niigata sake as a whole has come to be identified with the slogan *tanrei karaku-chi*, signifying a light, clean, dry style, and this example is certainly in that mold. Yet, rather than any marketing philosophy, it is the organic sense of this as a well-loved local regular brand, its crisp flavor unobtrusively matching regional tastes, that gives it its character.

Takashimizu, Seisen Karakuchi

BRAND: Takashimizu
TYPE: Regular
BREWERY: Akita Shurui Seizō, in Akita Prefecture

The main thrust of sake brewing in Akita has tradition-ally been sweet, and this perhaps explains why, rather than giving a direct sensation of dryness, the light touch of this sake makes it endlessly quaffable.

MINOR GENRES: NONE OF THE ABOVE

The following are fun, but you are less likely to come across them casually, since they are all found lurking on the fringes of the sake world. Many breweries have no products in the types introduced here. Some breweries, while not holding the patent, are strongly identified with one or other of these curiosities, as is the case with the first two sakes introduced below.

Kijōshu • "Noble-Brew Sake"

Most of the few producers of this rich, sweet style of sake age it before sale: the range of sensations can be reminiscent of sweet sherry, woody notes combining with hay and chocolate and rich berry flavors. The texture of all but the rare young examples is rich and oily, with amber, copper, and coffee colors.

In making *kijōshu*, finished sake is added to a still fermenting batch, bringing the fermentation to an early halt. There is a parallel with port wine, but there is no contest in terms of the antiquity of the techniques: kijōshu represents a revival of a method used in Japan a millennium ago.

SAKE REVIEW *KIJŌSHU*

Hanahato Kijōshu, 7-nen Chozō

BRAND: Hanahato
TYPE: Kijōshu
BREWERY: Enoki Shuzō, in Hiroshima Prefecture

This brewery is the first to have brought back the kijōshu style and placed it on the modern stage by adapting methods recorded in documents of the Heian period (794–1185). Sake is used instead of water in brewing, imparting a richly constituted flavor, raisin-like nuances within a strong treacly sweetness. This has been well aged to give it its characteristic brown color (page 25), and makes an excellent dessert wine or nightcap. Kijōshu is also finding new acclaim in the United States.

アルコール添加酒

Alcohol-Added Sake

During the hard years during and after World War II, severe food shortages in Japan made it necessary to find a way to make more sake with less rice. Even today, in line with techniques developed then, several bits and pieces may be added to the original pure-rice base to make lower grades of sake. When making Premium Sake, though, the only permitted addition is brewers' alcohol—a more or less neutral, distilled spirit. The technique had been known for a couple of hundred years before economic necessity (and government regulation) forced brewers to adopt it widely as a yield-boosting measure. The historical purpose of adding a spirit was to prevent spoiling, but it was found that sake to which alcohol had been added has a crisp, clean finish, and that the addition helped trap volatile aromatics in the finished sake to produce a more fragrant result.

Kodaishu • "Sake of Antiquity"

A number of breweries have dug around in old books and manuscripts and, following the methods of bygone centuries, have brewed up some interesting concoctions. The results are as varied and colorful as the methods themselves, but tend to the dark and funky.

Kodaimai-zukuri, Asamurasaki

BRAND: Kikusakari
TYPE: Kodaishu
BREWERY: Kiuchi Shuzō, in Ibaraki Prefecture

This visually appealing, rose-tinted sake (see page 25) has found a good reception with sake fans in New York. *Asamurasaki* is the name of the ancient black variety of rice used in brewing. There is a slight, thought-provoking scent of strawberry. A sweet-and-sour complex of flavors floods the palate, making this a better match for Western, rather than Japanese, food.

Taru-zake • Keg Sake

This sake is deliberately treated to give it the scent of wood. Traditionally, *taru-zake* is aged for a brief period in kegs (*taru*). This imparts the piquant fragrance of the cedar wood to the liquid.

Tokubetsu Junmai, Kin Taruhei

BRAND: Taruhei
TYPE: Taru-zake
BREWERY: Taruhei Shuzō, in Yamagata Prefecture

The fragrance of the wooden cask wafts up to meet the thick acidity that rises to fill the mouth. Because the flavor is so solid, there is a tendency for the wood fragrance to feel subdued. This is multilayered sake, which gives a strong impression of the ample umami flavors from the rice.

Sparkling Sake • *Happō-sei Seishu*

With a respectful bow to the pioneers who have been in this field for decades, today's sparkling sake is a new development. The recent activity has been partly related to the quest for tasty, low-alcohol sake. Not all carbonated sake is low-alcohol, however; you can find products in all ranges. The lighter styles are great as aperitifs, or for toasts, in familiar, bubbly fashion. You may come across bubbly genshu, and the combination of 17 or 18 percent alcohol with fizz makes for very heady drinking.

Hōhōshu

BRAND: Kamo Midori, Chikurin
TYPE: Sparkling sake
BREWERY: Marumoto Shuzō, in Okayama Prefecture

The little explosions of gas make a refreshing impression. This low-alcohol sake shows yogurt-like sweet-and-sour elements of taste and fragrance. Apart from the orthodox approach of drinking this well chilled, it is also fun to freeze it and enjoy it as sherbet. It goes well with spicey dishes.

chapter Three

On the Road
Breweries and Regions

Midwinter landscape. Sake brewing has been concentrated in the coldest part of the year for centuries. The cold winter air is clean and low in bacteria that could spoil the sake, and a low temperature helps the brewer control the pattern of fermentation.

It is always fun to drink the local brew while on the road in Japan. However, if you don't have that opportunity, you can whistle up a very good virtual tour with brands named for Japanese regions and landmarks.

Sake breweries—or *kura* in Japanese—are not just factories churning out plonk. They exist in the unique matrix of wider Japanese culture—a fact richly reflected in the enormous range of color and variety in the names of breweries and individual products. A Japanese person who comes across a brand name using the character for turtle, or the hexagonal kimono design that represents it, will automatically recall a specific series of associations. In particular, trees, foods, or colors all have a range of meanings when they occur. The aspirant to cultural fluency will find no more pleasant tutorial system than a course in sake names and labels, a true treasury of information about Japanese thought and values.

REGIONAL SAKE STYLES AND TRENDS

Until quite recently, most sake brands were consumed only locally, and were made to match the diet and lifestyle of their locality. Just as Japan's luxuriant regional dialects have paled as a result of greater social mobility and the influence of television, so the local color of the sake world has taken on new, sometimes paler shades. Yet, regional distinctions have not disappeared. People from the far north of Japan still appear on national news programs with subtitles, so that they might be understood by all despite their dialects. Moreover, people from Tokyo are still never sure whether people from Osaka are joking or not. And even today, sake from the chilly north still tastes different from that brewed in the warmer climes of western Japan.

◀ Aside from a tofu restaurant and an art gallery, Ozawa Shuzō's brewery compound (page 63) accommodates a 300-year-old thatched-roof farmhouse, where the owner and his family reside.

Eastern Sake, Western Sake

Sake brewed (and stored) in a warm environment has a richer, fuller, and earthier flavor than that of chillier regions. Climatic influences are reinforced in various ways. The regional brewers' guilds (discussed in the following pages) have each brought their own influence to bear. The most famous brewers' rice is Yamada Nishiki (page 81), hailing from Hyōgo in western Japan, and giving depth of flavor to the sake from which it is made. It does not thrive in the cold of eastern Japan, however, where the representative brewer's rice, Miyama Nishiki (page 82), gives light, fine-lined results.

Coastal Sake, Mountain Sake

Where fresh fish is easily available and an important part of the diet, the local brews tend to be light and dry to go with the delicate flavors of sashimi. Inland, fresh fish was a rarity until the era of refrigerated transportation—within living memory, in other words. In such areas, preserved foods, with much stronger, pungent flavors, were a vital part of the diet. For example, one of the specialties of the landlocked prefecture of Nara is *kaki no ha zushi*. This type of sushi is made with salt-pickled mackerel. Each piece is wrapped in a leaf (*ha*) of the persimmon (*kaki*) tree, which, having astringent properties, helps preserve the fish. In all inland areas, such strongly flavored, preserved food has been common out of necessity, and the sake that complements it is full-bodied and powerfully flavored. An extreme example of this is the notoriously pungent Shiga delicacy known as *funazushi*, which is so uncompromisingly odoriferous that only seriously, fat, funky koshu stands a chance with it.

Exceptions to Prove the Rule

Real life, of course, is too complicated to behave tidily, and to allow us to break sake down easily. Topographical quirks and the styles of individual breweries and master brewers (*tōji*) mean that there have always been exceptions to every rule that one might dream up to classify regional characteristics. In addition, new technology has come to allow producers to bypass factors that have traditionally had a defining effect on regional style. Using refrigeration, a producer in the warmer Kyushu area can age his sake at low temperatures. A brewer in Hokkaido can buy Yamada Nishiki rice from Hyōgo. No. 10 yeast, which originated in the Tōhoku region, is now nationally available. In one and the same prefecture—even amongst the products of the same brewery—it is now quite common to find distinctive styles in the low-end traditional products for sale in conservative local markets, as well as in the high-end segment of Premium Sake, until recently sold largely in urban markets.

Contemporary sake, for all these reasons, is marvellously varied and diverse. And yet, and yet—and thank heavens—the traditional regional color which grew up organically over the centuries is still there as an underlying theme to treasure and enjoy.

BREWERS' GUILDS AND THEIR STYLES

Tōji: The Master Brewers

For the best part of three hundred years, sake has been made by seasonally employed craftsmen. The symbiotic relationship between the breweries of Japan and the artisans of the brewing guilds is one of the industry's unique features. The master brewer is called a *tōji*, and the traditional guild system is known as the *tōji seido*—tōji system.

Origins of The *Tōji* System

In the Edo period, a combination of economic, technical, and political developments gave rise to the *kan-zukuri* system in which brewing was restricted to the coldest months of the year. At the same time, agricultural advances left the men in rural farming communities with time on their hands in the winter months, when their snowbound fields could provide them with no income. Thus these men came to leave their homes after the fall rice harvest to provide the seasonal manpower needed by sake breweries. Guilds were formed, taking on the name of the members' home region, and each guild developed its own style and jealously guarded its secrets. In time, the guilds took on formal structures and began to play the role of matchmaker, responding to requests from breweries for staff by introducing individual tōji. Technical information and brewing secrets passed from generation to generation, each master tutoring a successor. Later, the guilds also began to run study sessions in the off-season, schooling their members in the methods and mysteries of brewing.

The Role of the *Tōji*

The master brewer takes his trusted team with him to the brewery in the fall. This has traditionally meant that, when the tōji changes, so does the entire brewing staff.

As well as handling the technicalities of brewing, in the past the tōji also has been responsible for hiring and firing. This meant that master brewers were figures of great influence in their home regions. The veteran brewers with whom I first worked told me that, when they were young, it was still common for aspiring brewers to work the master brewer's rice fields before their own, so keen was the competition to work in the brewing season. Besides the economic incentive, going away to make sake was considered proof of manhood in their communities.

Brewery Life

Like many traditional Japanese enterprises, sake breweries are very conservative places. The hierarchy in a traditional brewery is very rigid. The tōji is referred

◄ Sake storage tanks. Wooden-framed brewery buildings have wattle-and-daub walls plastered white on the outside and roofed with heavy clay tiles, also on a bed of wattle-and-daub. All that mud and straw makes excellent insulation. The white exterior reflects the searing sunlight of the Japanese summer, and the thick roof and walls act as a buffer against the heat. Temperature changes very slowly inside, making an ideal environment for aging sake.

to as Oya-san (from *oyaji*, meaning father); and the workers below him are known collectively as *kurabito* (literally, brewery people). Besides mastering the technical difficulties of brewing, a master brewer needs to be a skilful manager of people in order to keep the team working smoothly throughout the intense months of communal living during the brewing season.

In the past, the aspiring young brewer would start work at the bottom of the ladder, doing the cooking. (There was no "women's work," since women were traditionally forbidden to enter sake breweries in order to avoid incurring the jealous anger of the sake divinity.) He might also be assigned to help out in the kōji culture room between times, where a key part of the brewing process takes place (see page 85). As time went on, he would progress to the washing of equipment (an unending task in a brewery), then on to care of the tools themselves, before eventually moving up to one of the stages of brewing proper.

The elite amongst the kurabito are the three workers in charge of the yeast starter—the kōji and the fermenting mash. These three eminences are known as *sannyaku*—a term for three of the highest ranks of sumo wrestler. The last of these three is known as *kashira* (written with the character for part of the anatomy, the head). He is the tōji's right hand, responsible for directing the practical daily business of brewing.

The Guilds Today

In recent years, rural communities have experienced a preview of the problems associated with the graying of society that are soon to be faced by Japan as a whole. Without exception, the guilds are faced with severe shortages of young blood—just as the rural communities from which they hail are struggling to find sufficient young people to farm the land in the next generation.

When I started brewing, it was my privilege to work in the company of a veteran team, working and living in the brewery as had their fathers and their fathers'

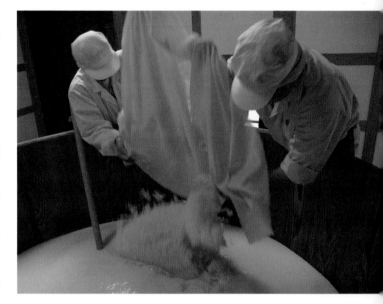

Adding the ingredients at the mashing stage.

fathers before them; they are now all retired. Although there are still active teams comprised entirely of veterans from the traditional guilds, breweries are being forced to find new sources of labor. There are already many breweries that have decades of experience in brewing using locally employed staff rather than seasonal kurabito, just as they may have a university-trained technician (*gishi*) rather than a tōji as the person ultimately responsible for brewing.

Increasing the number of full-time staff is a heavy financial burden for smaller breweries, however, and for many the manpower problem is far from solved. A growing number of these breweries are adopting a hybrid system, with a master brewer from one of the traditional guilds supervising a staff of locally employed company employees. The result is people like me, who are affiliated to traditional regional guilds, but who do not hail from the brewery's home area. This provides an important channel for transmitting the wisdom of the many great veteran brewers.

Another increasingly common occurrence is that the owner of a small brewery plays the role of tōji himself—or herself. A number of breweries have female tōji, and still more have women working in other capacities—though the sake world is still male-dominated.

A selection of prominent brewers' guilds and their styles are discussed in the following pages, under the headings of their home regions. There are also brief introductions to those breweries whose products are reviewed in this book. The order is geographical, from north to south.

► Stirring the fermenting sake.

SAKE COUNTRY

A Region by Region Tour

NOTE: Sake and brewery reviews were written by Haruo Matsuzaki, with translations by the author.

Aomori Prefecture

BRAND: Denshu
BREWERY: Nishida Shuzō-ten

This firm originally brewed under the name Kikuizimi. The Denshu brand (written with the characters for rice field and sake) was chosen to express the concept of junmai sake brewed to give full expression to flavors from the rice. Thirty years on from its debut, it has grown into an unshakably popular name, with a record of numerous top places in contests and magazine questionnaires. The firm's painstaking people-heavy approach and commitment to hand-brewing have earned it great respect from other producers, and its success is firmly based on rock-solid brewing practice.

Denshu Tokubetsu Junmaishu

BRAND: Denshu
TYPE: Tokubetsu junmai
BREWERY: Nishida Shuzō-ten

Light, with the gentlest sweetness, excellent texture on the palate, and a total lack of distracting flavors, the strength of this sake is its softness and an immensely fine structure. The silky refinement of touch is certainly one element in this sake's popularity, and a trademark of the style of the Nanbu school of brewers (see page 59).

JAPAN AND ITS PREFECTURES

HOKKAIDO

• Sapporo

JAPAN SEA

• Sendai

• Tokyo

• Kyoto
Osaka

• Fukuoka

SHIKOKU

KYŪSHŪ

PACIFIC OCEAN

Akita Prefecture

This prefecture has long advertised its sake with the slogan *bishu ōkoku*, or the Kingdom of Fine Sake. The fourth-most prolific sake producer, this is one of the few prefectures to boast a regional sake research institute. The development of the ginjō yeast AK–1 in 1990 is the institute's greatest coup of recent decades, and the resulting elegant brews reaped a plentiful harvest of gold medals in the National Assessment for New Sake in 1991. The sought-after new strain of yeast finally became generally available to the nation's brewers when it was marketed as Association Yeast No. 15 in 1996. In addition to being admired for its new yeast by the nation's sake fans, the prefecture also enjoys a large and loyal local following of serious sake drinkers for more traditional, low-end products.

BRAND: Ama no To (also Heaven's Door)
BREWERY: Asamai Shuzō

This brewery has worked energetically in order to be able to brew exclusively with locally produced brewers' rice, forming a study group with local farmers—one of whom is the master brewer. Product names reflect the company's pride in being a truly local producer from Akita, one of the nation's most famous rice-growing regions. *Sake on page 36.*

酒の名前

Themes for Sake Names
① Trees and Plants

Many plants have special significance in the Japanese scheme of things, and consequently appear often in names and on labels. The auspicious trinity of pine, bamboo, and plum is known to sake lovers as the brand name of the giant Takara brewery, *Shōchikubai*, and the trio crops up in many brand names, in combination or as separate components. Other frequent fliers are *sakura* (the cherry, the blossoms of which are the national flower) and *kiku* (the chrysanthemum, which is the emblem of the imperial family). The botanically minded drinker can also find peonies (botan), cedar (sugi), orchids (ran), the *katsura* tree, and rice-related brand names by the bushel.

Some Plant and Flower Sake Names

Kiku Masamune
  (Chrysanthemum Masamune)
Sakura Masamune (Cherry Masamune)
Koshi no Kanbai
  (Winter Plum of Niigata, page 37)
Secchu-bai (Plum in the Snow)
Haku Botan (White Peony)
Kome Hyappyō (A Hundred Bales of Rice)
Inada Hime (Paddyfield Princess)
Kinkan Kuromatsu (Gold Crown Pine)

Sakura Masamune

Haku Botan

BRAND: Hiraizumi
BREWERY: Hiraizumi Honpo

Founded in the fifteenth century, this venerable company boasts the third-longest history of any brewery. Originally a cargo company based in southern Osaka (then called the Land of Izumi), the concern settled in Hirazawa in Akita, where it owned warehouses. The brand name unites elements from the name of the company's original and present homes. That the firm has brewed here successfully since the distant days of its founding is due in no small part to its being blessed with water of a hardness rarely matched in Japan. Hiraizumi's skill in the yamahai method of brewing is also a result of this. The dense construction of the sake, rich in acidity, makes for a house style quite distinct from other Akita brews.

Yamahai Junmaishu, Hiraizumi

BRAND: Hiraizumi
TYPE: Yamahai junmai
BREWERY: Hiraizumi Honpo

With acidity as the focal point, this is wrapped in bitter, astringent, and other flavor elements to give a complexly constructed whole. Also showing varied aromatic elements—grains and nuts—the overall effect maintains a gentle, well-matured feeling.

BRAND: Takashimizu
BREWERY: Akita Shurui Seizō

A number of breweries in the area of contemporary Akita city merged to form this company during World War II. Despite having opened for business only after the war, the brand has become not only one of the most famous of the many household names from the Akita brewing powerhouse, but also one of the top handful of labels in eastern Japan in terms of production volume. The company currently has two active breweries. *Sake on page 49.*

Iwate Prefecture

BREWERS' GUILD: Nanbu Tōji

Despite being home to the most populous brewers' guild in Japan, Iwate Prefecture has only a handful of breweries in which they can work. As a consequence, members of the Nanbu guild work widely throughout Eastern Japan. As numbers in some of the guilds in western Japan have dwindled, the Nanbu brewers have filled many of the gaps, meaning that more are active further west than was traditionally the case. The signature style of the Nanbu school is light and crisp, and ginjō made by its member tends to the elegantly fragrant.

Yamagata Prefecture

The Yamagata region is home to a swathe of the *ji-zake* world's most respected, popular, and successful names. The development and marketing of a "prefecture brand" has become a familiar strategy across the nation. In this sense, Yamagata's *Dewa 33* (*Dewa San San*) series is not unusual. However, the series's policy of using the specially developed Dewa Sansan brewer's rice (same reading, different characters), an original yeast strain, and even a proprietary strain of kōji spores (Yamagata oryzae) bespeaks a rare thoroughness of purpose. Overall, the region's style can stand as a paradigm of the Premium products of the Tōhoku region—crisp, limpid, fragrant sake.

BRAND: Dewazakura
BREWERY: Dewazakura Shuzō

The reasonably priced *Ōka* (page 39) sake contributed to the expansion of the fledgling ginjō market, and continues its long-selling run today. Dewazakura also sells a large proportion of sake unpasteurized, and uses cooling equipment for all its storage tanks and in-the-bottle pasteurizing to achieve fresh and refreshing flavor. With a hands-on, labor-intensive policy for everything including the transportation of steamed rice and kōji, it is fair to say that a thoroughgoing commitment to hand-brewing is responsible for the smoothness of the sake.

BRANDS: Shōnai Homare, Eikō Fuji
BREWERY: Fuji Shuzō

This brewery is one of the grand old men in the famous Shōnai brewing region. In the Edo period, the brewing industry in the Oyama district of Tsuruoka flourished to the extent that it became known as the Nada of Tōhoku (see page 72). The sake is characterized by graceful lines and umami flavor combining with a soft touch on the palate. The expression of the fine qualities of No. 10 yeast is intrinsic to the style. The dai ginjō product *Koshuya no Hitoriyogari* (which uses the same yeast) is the company's flagship product. *Another Fuji Shuzō sake is on page 86.*

BRAND: Taruhei
BREWERY: Taruhei Shuzō

If small, provincial breweries are to survive, they cannot dance to the same music as national brands. This firm danced its first solo steps more than forty years ago, when it began brewing traditional, dry, pure-rice sake, and aging it for a fixed period in wooden kegs to impart the scent of the wood. Shipping such dry products as the Sumiyoshi line, and such rich-flavored labels as the Taruhei series, the company's unique, character-rich products are perennially popular. The brewer is also much admired for the wealth of flavor found in those of its sakes made with Yamada Nishiki rice (which in the beginning, was extremely hard for northern breweries to obtain). Currently, pure-rice sake accounts for more than 80 percent of the company's production. *Sake on page 51.*

Themes for Sake Names
② Animals, Real and Imaginary

In Japan, certain birds and animals have particular significance, such as the crane and the turtle, which are symbols of good fortune and longevity, respectively. (According to proverbs, the crane is said to live a thousand years and the turtle ten thousand.) "Crane" brands are right up there with the "mountain" brands as the most numerous, and are often linked with regional name tags. Though not to the extent of the flocks of cranes that adorn sake labels across the country, there are, nevertheless, a large number of "turtle" brands. Deer have auspicious mythical associations in Japan, and there is also a tradition, imported from China, relating them to longevity, so there are a large number of "deer" sakes, too.

Many legendary creatures lend their names and auras to sake brands, including long-nosed *tengu* demons, and *oni* goblins. These last range from impish to ogre-like, and star in any number of folktales. Beer drinkers know the fabled beast *kirin*; it also crops up in the sake world, as does the phoenix. The many dragon names were chosen for their associations with power.

Other birds, fish, and animals celebrated as sake brands include the auspicious carp (*koi*) and sea bream (*tai*), horses, bush warblers, hawks, whales, doves, cows, and lions.

Animals and Bird Sake Brands

Saijo Tsuru ("Saijo Crane," the famous Hiroshima brewing center)
Tosa Tsuru (Tosa Crane)
Haku Tsuru (White Crane)
Yama Tsuru (Mountain Crane)
Kino Tsuru (Crane of Ki)
Hoku Shika (Northern Deer)
Aki Shika (Autumn Deer)
Haru Shika (Spring Deer)
Haku Shika (White Deer)
Haku Taka (White Hawk, page 80)
Ten Taka (Heavenly Hawk)
Kin Kame (Golden Turtle)
Shin Kame (Divine Turtle, page 63)
Taki no Koi (Carp in the Waterfall)
Yuki Suzume (Sparrow in the Snow)
Naruto Tai (Naruto Bream, page 74)
Shishi no Sato (Lion's Lair)

Mythical Creatures

Oni Koroshi (Demon Slayer)
Tengu Mai (Goblin Dance)
Koku Ryū (Black Dragon, page 39)
Azuma Ryū (Eastern Dragon)
O-tori Zakura (Phoenix Cherry)

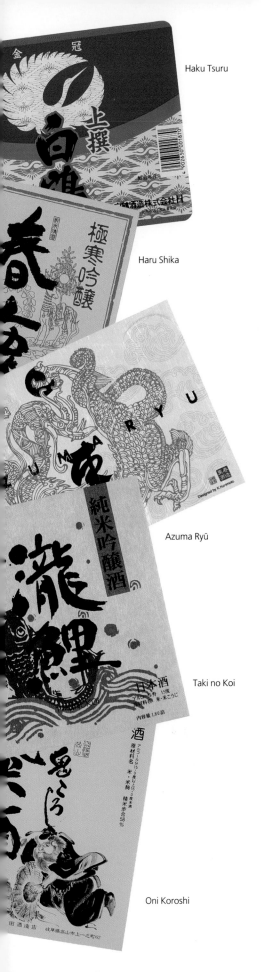

Haku Tsuru

Haru Shika

Azuma Ryū

Taki no Koi

Oni Koroshi

Miyagi Prefecture

BRAND: Ichi no Kura
BREWERY: Ichi no Kura

This company was born when four medium-sized Miyagi producers joined forces in 1973. This extremely young brewery soon showed itself to be abreast, or even ahead, of the times when it shifted production of its main brands to Premium level, and can now be said to have built itself a strong base as a highly popular name. It maintains its forward-looking stance today with low-alcohol products like Himezen and the sparkling, lightly cloudy Suzune that was developed at the suggestion of female staff members. These brands not only helped invent the low-alcohol genre, but they remain top-selling products in the field. *Sake on page 45.*

BRAND: Urakasumi
BREWERY: Saura

The Urakasumi style—a soft yet fragrant sake made with local rice—is said not only to have given birth to one form of ginjō brewing, but also to have shaped the practices of the Nanbu guild of brewers (page 59). The Urakasumi name is known as a champion, not only of the Tōhoku region, but of all eastern Japan. *Sake on page 39.*

Fukushima Prefecture

Fukushima is a good prefectural example of the folly of reductive explanations of regional style. Although not one of the prefectures generally thought of as a major producing region, it is in fact safely in the top ten, with around ninety breweries both great and small. The most prolific brewing area is that around Aizu Wakamatsu city, where about forty breweries are to be found, with about twenty within the city itself. This inland part of the prefecture has cold winters with heavy snowfalls, and the sake made here tends to be hearty and full-flavored. Wing over to the Pacific coast, and you find a region with mild winters, where the sake is drier and lighter. That this kind of sake goes well with the delicate flavors of freshly landed sashimi is, of course, no coincidence.

Like a number of other prefectures, Fukushima has recently seen plenty of action from a locally developed yeast strain, in this case Yume Kōbo—Dream Yeast.

BRAND: Daishichi
BREWERY: Daishichi Shuzō

This brewery was a leader in popularizing and adapting the venerable kimoto technique to modern tastes. Its introduction of the *henpei* ("flat") mode of rice polishing (milling along the breadth rather than the length of the grain) allows the brewery to polish more efficiently, and so produce a clean sake with low levels of amino acids. *Sake on page 43.*

BRAND: Oku no Matsu
BREWERY: Oku no Matsu Shuzō

This is a highly regarded brewery in central Fukushima Prefecture that makes sake using local rice, local water, and local people. The brewery's run of six successive Gold Medals in the National Assessment for New Sake is just one result of its proud record of rock-solid technical expertise. The firm is also an active exporter (to the United States, Canada, Taiwan, Hong Kong, and other destinations) and an energetic promoter of the cultural aspects of sake. *Sake on page 36.*

 BRAND: Suehiro
BREWERY: Suehiro Shuzō

The Aizu region in Fukushima Prefecture is famous for rice production, and this brewery has contracts for its raw materials with around one hundred farms. In a region where sweet sake is the rule, this company developed a range of products showing great variety, including polished nama and dai ginjō sakes. *Sake on page 37.*

 BRAND: Yamatogawa (also Yauemon, Tsuki Akari, Rashiku)
BREWERY: Yamatogawa Shuzō-ten

This is a long-established business in Kitakata city, famous for the many remaining beautiful traditional storehouse buildings. In 1990, the company began production in a new brewery in the city outskirts, and transformed its historical brewery buildings into a museum housing an exhibition of traditional brewing implements.

Situated in one of the top rice-producing regions in the Tōhoku area, the company is involved in the entire scope of sake production, commencing with rice growing. The Yamada Nishiki grown in the brewery-owned fields is used to make dai ginjō. *Sake on page 44.*

Ibaraki Prefecture

 BRAND: Kikusakari
BREWERY: Kiuchi Shuzō

With a brewing staff consisting mainly of full-time company employees in their twenties, this is one of the most youthful breweries in the country. Kikusakari has rice-growing contracts with local farmers, and began to diversify it products with the launch of Hitachino Nest Beer in 1996. The brewery's products include *shōchū* spirit, wine made from grapes in a vineyard behind the brewery, and yuzu wine. The company exploits its small batch size by allowing consumers to experience brewing hands on, and this is another reason for the brewery's popularity. *Sake on page 51.*

▶ The Oku Tama region, Tokyo Prefecture. The mountainous Japanese landscape is blessed with bountiful supplies of fresh water, an essential ingredient for fine sake.

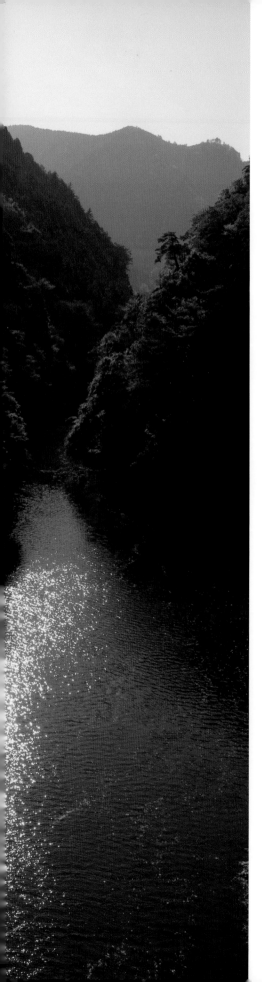

Saitama Prefecture

BRAND: Shinkame
BREWERY: Shinkame Shuzō

Brewing solely pure-rice sake, Shinkame is highly respected not only by sake fans, but also specialist retailers and other brewers. Despite the current fashion for fresh, fragrant styles, this brewery has insisted on a generous aging period, reflecting its commitment to making sake with deep, complex flavor. Although the company also uses No. 9 yeast to make dai ginjō, it continues to develop products using No. 7 yeast (rarely used in ginjō brewing) as part of its championing of solid, unostentatious flavors.

Tokyo Prefecture

BRAND: Sawa no I
BREWERY: Ozawa Shuzō

Located some 37 miles (60 kilometers) from central Tokyo, this kura is set in beautiful, natural, verdant valley surroundings. The superb water welling up in the tunnel-like well bored horizontally into the mountain face behind the brewery is the keystone of the crisp, uncluttered lines of Sawa no I brand sake. The brewery's offerings have gained added cachet from its specialty tofu restaurant Mamagotaya, as well as the Kanzashi Art Gallery, both of which are run by the brewery in nearby locations overlooking superb views of the Tama river valley.

Sawa no I, Junmai Dai-karakuchi

BRAND: Sawa no I
TYPE: Junmai
BREWERY: Ozawa Shuzō

A refreshing fragrance flits across the palate first, followed by a light aftertaste that leaves a dry impression and keeps things tight. The flavor is smooth and without distractions, making this taut, extra-dry sake excellent at a wide range of temperatures and with many styles of food: one that invites a refill.

Kanagawa Prefecture

BRAND: Izumibashi
BREWERY: Izumibashi Shuzō

This company does business in a corner of the town of Ebina, which, only 31 miles (50 kilometers) from central Tokyo, is expanding as a bedroom town. Besides growing such prized strains of brewing rice as Yamada Nishiki and Omachi in the surrounding rice fields owned by the brewery, the company has also made an energetic appeal to local farmers to ensure a supply of locally grown rice. *Sake on page 36.*

Yamanashi Prefecture

BRAND: Shichiken
BREWERY: Yamanashi Meijō

This brewery is at the eastern foot of the Southern Alps. The area is famous for its water, which has also lured a national whiskey distiller to the region. Shichiken sakes share a light, bracing quality with a clean flavor reflecting the characteristics of the mineral-light soft water. The company has growing contracts with local farmers for Miyama Nishiki brewers' rice, and is enthusiastically involved in rice production.

Charming buildings that were a retreat for the Emperor Meiji, a tasting area, and brewery-run restaurant make this company a popular destination for tourists. *Sake on page 41.*

Shizuoka Prefecture

BRAND: Kaiun (also Takatenjin)
BREWERY: Doi Shuzō-jō

From state-of-the-art rice polishing equipment to enormous refrigerated storage warehouses, this company's unstinting investment in ginjō production has given us the most elegant of sakes. The harvest has not been confined to ginjō sake, however, as the whole range of Kaiun products have enjoyed a growing reputation. This brewery was also one of the driving forces behind the emergence of the Shizuoka region as a new star in the 1980s. The extremely auspicious name, Kaiun (meaning impending good fortune), and its similarly auspicious packaging, makes this sake a popular choice in the formal gift-giving seasons.

Kaiun, Dai Ginjō

BRAND: Kaiun
TYPE: Dai ginjō   **BRAND:** Kaiun
BREWERY: Doi Shuzō-jō

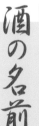

Wreathed in refreshing pear and apple fragrance, the smooth opening and the swift cleanliness of the finish offer a superb balance. The clean clarity and low acidity of Kaiun's dai ginjō is the quintessence of sake from Shizuoka, a prefecture that, with an extensive coastline, is blessed with fine fresh seafood, for which this sake is a perfect complement.

BRAND: Eikun
BREWERY: Eikun Shuzō

Despite being a small brewery, Eikun insists on polishing rice in-house. As well as using the rice-washing and kōji-making equipment developed by Shizuoka Prefecture, it has also made many ingenious adjustments of its own to the brewing process.

Themes for Sake Names
③ People: Historical and Legendary Figures

All kinds of people from history and legend have been immortalized in sake brand names. On a contemporary note, there are also plenty of brands that have been named for their creators—the name of a famous master brewer, or the brewery owner.

Rihaku (boozy Chinese Poet Li-Po, page 75)
Benkei (legendary warrior monk)
Sharaku (legendary ukiyo-e artist)
Santōka (poet and all-round cultural icon)
Daruma Masamune (named for Daruma, founder of Zen Buddhism)
Jūyon-dai (fourteenth generation—referring to the number of generations this Yamagata company has been brewing, although the current brewer is fifteenth in line)

Benkei

Sharaku

Eikun, Dai Ginjō Iroha

BRAND: Eikun
TYPE: Dai ginjō
BREWERY: Eikun Shuzō

This firm has made skilled use of M-310 yeast, using it to make some dai ginjō products and sake for entry in regional and national contests. The yeast gives a fragrance that bursts on the palate. The base for this sake is the light, lissom Shizuoka style of sake, given extra flair by the fragrance, which leads the way. The presence of the aroma is the defining accent, throwing a particularly fresh feeling into focus.

Niigata Prefecture

A recent reader's poll conducted by a men's magazine had no less than three Niigata brands in the top five most popular sake brands. The style that has pushed the prefecture to the number three spot in terms of volume produced is *tanrei karakuchi*, the light, dry, crisp style that was the height of fashion for a number of years. This is the region in which most of the ultra-famous brands have made their reputations, but the region offers surprising variety for those inclined to look. The technical skill of the region's brewers is regularly proven with a great stack of gold medals in the annual national contest. Niigata has more breweries than any prefecture but Hyōgo.

BREWERS' GUILD: Echigo Tōji

This guild has the second-largest membership after the Nanbu guild. Any sake fan asked about Niigata will come up with the expression tanrei karakuchi, and the tōji hailing from the region are certainly skilled in the style. The Echigo guild's members are active primarily in their home prefecture, with a scattering elsewhere.

BRAND: Kiyoizumi
BREWERY: Kusumi Shuzō

This brewery is famous for having resurrected the dormant rice variety Kame no O, and its continuing energetic cooperation with local farmers shows its determination to maintain its position as the original champion of the strain, even as a growing number of other brewers begin to use it. Overall, the Kusumi brewery makes sake reminiscent of the clear spring water that the name Kiyoizumi signifies. *Sake on page 83.*

BRAND: Hakkaisan
BREWERY: Hakkai Jōzō

This brand shot to fame early as an incarnation of the Niigata tanrei karakuchi style. In order to express and sustain their light, fluid approach, the Hakkaisan people lifted the level of polish of the raw materials, and took care to provide an ideal, low-temperature storage environment (below 60° F/15° C) for all their products, from the top-class brews down to their "regular" products. The company completed a new factory in 2004 and continues to work to improve product quality and reliability. *Sake on page 49.*

 BRAND: Kikusui
BREWERY: Kikusui Shuzō

One of the top three producers in the prefecture, Kikusui is among Niigata's best-known "faces." The nationwide popularity of its style—light and limpid in the representative Niigata fashion—was triggered by the full-flavored Funaku-chi sake that, in its distribution-friendly aluminum can, truly can be said to have been a pioneering product in the marketing of unpasteurized sake. With its recent extension of the 300-milliliter-size product range, and development of a junmai ginjō sake made with organic rice, the company is attracting new fans. *Sake on page 42.*

 BRAND: Kirin (also Kanbara)
BREWERY: Kaetsu Shuzō

Even in a region that boasts the driest sakes, this area is known for its dry brews, and the brewery reflects the tradition of making clean, blemish-free products with a swift, incisive finish. The recently introduced Kanbara line marks a depar-ture from the traditional stance, with a series of more fully flavored products.

The brewery's last two generations of *kuramoto* spent time working as sake specialists in the Appraisal Section of the Taxation Bureau, as a result of which they brought a wealth of academic expertise to the wide range of the company's brewing, and contributed to the polished quality of Kirin sake. *Sake on page 46.*

 BRAND: Koshi no Kanbai
BREWERY: Ishimoto Shuzō

About forty years ago, the Koshi no Kanbai name became nationally known as a dry sake at a time when such a thing was a rarity, and won fame as a sought-after "sake of dreams"—*maboroshi no sake*. Not only famous as the brand that triggered the ji-zake boom, it has also played a central role as the force driving the popularity of Niigata Prefecture as a sake-producing region. *Sake on page 37.*

 BRAND: Yoshinogawa
BREWERY: Yoshinogawa

This company has mastered the use of Niigata's long-selling brewers' rice, Gohyaku-man-goku, using it to give an intricate, understated flavor quite different from that of Yamada Nishiki sake. Recently, quite a stir has been made with the Kurabito Aijōshu series (a play on the words for "love" and "brewed with love"), which is made using Gohyakuman-goku grown by the brewing staff. The house style of light-drinking, translucent sake is truly the embodiment of the Niigata school.

Yoshinogawa Dai Ginjō

BRAND: Yoshinogawa
TYPE: Dai ginjō
BREWERY: Yoshinogawa

A regular prize-winner at the various trade contests, this brand is representative of the Echigo style. Clear lines and clean, uncluttered flavor combine with fragrances of apple and ripe melon to give a vibrant impression. The assured flavor with its clean finish make this a dai ginjō that goes well with food.

Nagano Prefecture

BRAND: Kikuhide
BREWERY: Kitsukura Shuzō

"Alps" Yeast was developed by Nagano Prefecture and, with its ability to produce a high, fruity fragrance, is now used by producers across the nation and yields regular prize winners in the national contest for new sake. It is not distinguished solely by its flowery top notes, but also by a well-tensioned quality, ripe with clear tangy acidity. This particular brewery skillfully utilizes the character of the yeast, using it to brew fine sake with breadth of rounded, rich flavor. As well as using local rice for its perennially popular junmai products, the company also makes the popular shōchū spirit *Mine* with Nagano-grown buckwheat.

Kikuhide, Dai Ginjō Kura

BRAND: Kikuhide
TYPE: Dai ginjō
BREWERY: Kitsukura Shuzō

This dry dai ginjō, wreathed in elegant apple scents, combines a charismatic crispness of high fragrance with a swift, clean finish. With excellent crisp texture on the palate, the overall image is one of polished refinement.

BRAND: Masumi
BREWERY: Miyasaka Jōzō

Association Yeast No. 7, with its settled aromatics and rock steady fermentation, was discovered in this brewery in 1946. Since then, Masumi's seamless, graceful style has made it one of Nagano's most famous representatives, a truly great brewery. The firm has opened a well-received shop, Cella Masumi, next door to the brewery, offering lifestyle suggestions with sake goods. *Sake on page 41.*

◄ The paddyfield landscape: a definitive Japanese view.

Gifu Prefecture

BRAND: Miyo-zakura
BREWERY: Miyo-zakura Jōzō

This brewery is in Ōta, a town that flourished as a staging post on the old Nakasendō highway connecting Ōmi (now Shiga Prefecture) and the capital (then known as Edo). The old-fashioned brewery buildings, giving a sense of the town's history, are part of the company's appeal.

The master brewer is only thirty years old but, with a Gold Medal in the Annual National Assessment for New Sake, he is firmly continuing the traditional model of brewing. *Sake on page 45.*

Toyama Prefecture

BRAND: Masuizumi
BREWERY: Masuda Shuzō-ten

One of the great breweries of the Hokuriku region, this company has been a leading player since the time of the ginjō boom. The master brewer Sanpai Koichi is held to be one of the Noto grouping's greatest (see the following guild entry), and the elegant sake made under his leadership has entranced fans. The refreshing, fruity, crystal clear aromatics are in the classical mold of sake from the north. With a Noto successor safely on board, we can be assured that Masuizumi will continue ginjō brewing in the same exquisite fashion.

This brewery has also recently undertaken ambitious projects to develop in new directions, such as the production of richly-flavored junmai dai ginjō made using a high proportion of kōji, and sake matured in wine casks from the French region of Burgundy. *Sake on page 41.*

Ishikawa Prefecture

Hanging off one end of this prefecture is the remote Noto Peninsula. The farmers and fishermen who live here form the backbone of the Noto Brewer's Guild, and their style defines the identity of the region's sake. The well-regarded Kanazawa Yeast developed here is on sale nationally as Association Yeast No. 14, but remains particularly popular with Ishikawa breweries.

BREWERS' GUILD: Noto Tōji

This guild is mainly active in its home prefecture, and in the region between Tokyo and Osaka—particularly Shiga, Shizuoka, and Fukui prefectures. The Noto style of sake is rich, soft, and full-bodied. Skill with the yamahai style of making the yeast starter (see pages 86–87) is one of the guild's trademarks, and some of the yamahai genre's most famous practitioners hail from here.

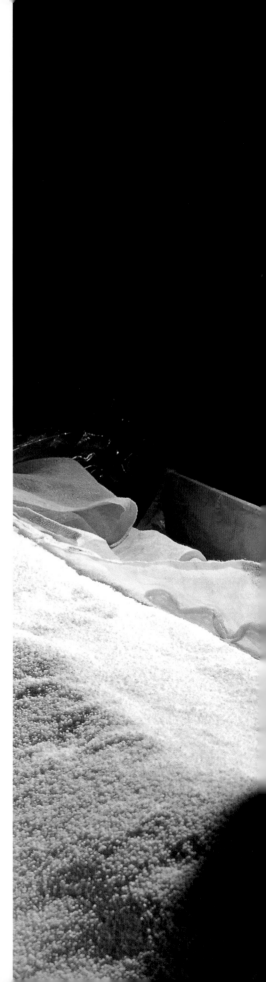

 BRANDS: Fukumasamune, Momotose, Kaga Tobi, Kuro Obi
BREWERY: Fukumitsuya

Aside from the traditional Fukumasamune (a great sake name from the Hokuriku district), this company has a colorful array of brand names (such as Kaga Tobi and Kuro Obi), each of which it has matched to the concept and style of the sake for which it was chosen. The all-encompassing characteristic of the brews is a full, rich, complex feeling, and the company excels in making sake that goes well with food, as befits a brewer that has matured in the grand old city of Kanazawa, with its tradition of culinary excellence. The company is taking steps to promote exports, and runs a restaurant and sake bar/store (Sake Shop Fukumitsuya) in Tokyo's Ginza district. *Sake on page 46.*

 BRAND: Chikuha
BREWERY: Kazuma Shuzō

Situated in the center of the Noto peninsula, this company brews lovely, elegant sake with a clean finish. *Sake on page 19.*

Fukui Prefecture

 BRAND: Ippongi
BREWERY: Ippongi Kubo Honten

Ippongi is in Katsuyama city, in the center of an area held to be one of the best for growing Gohyakuman-goku rice. The brewery has a steady following, making full use of the local rice to give an unostentatious feel with a core of solid flavor. As sake breweries go, this has a short history, only having changed from the manufacture of silk thread to that of sake in 1902. Introducing enamel tanks and refrigeration soon after, the company polished its brewing techniques while putting modern equipment in place, and has evolved into Fukui Prefecture's largest sake producer and one of the Hokuriku region's representative sake names. *Sake on page 83.*

 BRAND: Kokuryū
BREWERY: Kokuryū Shuzō

The Kokuryū (Black Dragon) brand name is famous and stands out even among the products of other sake brewers in the Hokuriku region, which is known as a leading ginjō-producing area. The company enjoys great popularity for the high quality of not only its costlier products, but also its lower priced labels. *Sake on page 39.*

◄ Kōji making: the crux of a sake brewer's labors.

Aichi Prefecture

BRAND: Kamoshibito Kuheiji (also Kuheiji, Niné)
BREWERY: Banjō Jōzō

The kuramoto here (still in his thirties) called in a high-school friend to be brewer, and the two work energetically in close collaboration to brew opulently flavored sake. A wealth of fruit-like fragrance and ripe taste is the overriding impression.

The original brand was Banjō, named after the company, but the talked-about new line, Kamoshibito Kuheiji, has become popular with izakaya and specialist retailers, and has also been exported to France. Kuheiji is the hereditary name assumed by each owner of the brewery once he reaches his prime. *Sake on page 48.*

Shiga Prefecture

BRAND: Biwa no Chōju
BREWERY: Ikemoto Shuzō

The earliest Shiga brewery to begin ginjō brewing and boasting an excellent record in the Assessment for New Sake, this company has become nationally famous as one of the great breweries of the Kinki region. *Sake on page 40.*

Kyoto Prefecture

Fushimi

If the crisp, dry Nada *otoko-zake* (masculine sake) is the sake world's yang, then the softer brews of Fushimi are surely its yin. The local water plays a decisive role; the wells of Fushimi are famous for their soft water. The resulting Fushimi trademark is soft, full, sweet sake. Around 90 percent of Kyoto's breweries are concentrated in this one tiny area of Kyoto.

BRANDS: Momo no Shizuku, Hinode Zakari
BREWERY: Matsumoto Shuzō

This medium-sized company relocated to the brewing mecca of Fushimi from its original location in eastern Kyoto. Even in the context of the kura-filled cityscape of Fushimi, its riverside wooden buildings make it one of the most picturesque of prospects. It makes an especially beautiful sight when the yellow rape flowers are in bloom in spring. As a member of the Pure Saké Association (Junsui Nihonshu Kyōkai), the brewery's pure-rice sake offers great variety. Its other main brand is Sawaya Matsumoto. Overall, the brewery makes smooth sake that blossoms on the palate, reflecting the strengths of the soft water used for brewing. *Sake on page 71.*

▶ Rice being sun-dried on tripods after harvest.

Junmai Ginjō, Momo no Shizuku

 BRAND: Momo no Shizuku
TYPE: Junmai ginjō
BREWERY: Matsumoto Shuzō

Momo no Shizuku literally means droplets from a peach, a phrase taken from a traditional Japanese *waka* poem about the Fushimi area. The sake is as fruity as the phrase suggests, and its clean, light feeling on the palate gives a harmonious impression. Neither too dry nor too sweet, the median flavors make this a versatile companion to food.

 BRAND: Tama no Hikari
BREWERY: Tama no Hikari Shuzō

This company specialises in brewing full-flavored junmai ginjō, making full use of fine rice from several regions, including Omachi from Okayama Prefecture, Yamada Nishiki from Hyōgo, and Okuhomare from Fukui. Having promoted pure-rice sake for the past forty years (since the days when the brewing of triple sake with added alcohol and sugars was standard), the company also played a central role in the foundation of The Pure Saké Association. The company began exporting sake early, and its products are currently on sale in the United States, Taiwan, Hong Kong, and Singapore. Its ji-zake is one of the most popular available overseas. *Sake on page 43.*

 BRAND: Tsuki no Katsura
BREWERY: Masuda Tokubei Shōten

Inevitably, when discussing this brewery, one starts with nigori-zake. Characterized by a fresh, fizzy flavor, the house nigori—a pioneer in the field and unbeatably popular in the four decades it has been on sale—was developed according to advice given by the legendary authority on brewing science, Kinichiro Sakaguchi. The company was early to market aged sake—its *Kohaku Hikari* (Amber Glow) sake is aged in ceramic containers—and it uses the historical Kyoto brewers' rice strain, Iwai, in contemporary brewing. The brewery offers a product range rich in variety. *Sake on page 47.*

Nara Prefecture

 BRAND: Ume no Yado, Tsuki Usagi
BREWERY: Ume no Yado Shuzō

With an overall average milling ratio of below 60 percent, and pure-rice sake representing more than half its production, this brewery is intensely focused on quality and has a wide range of products, particularly in the ginjō range. The sparkling low-alcohol sake *Tsuki Usagi* (Moon Rabbit, named for the rabbit which is pounding rice cakes on the moon) is also proving very popular. *Sake on page 82.*

Osaka Prefecture

BRAND: Rikyūbai (also Tōzai, Mukune, Root of Innocence)
BREWERY: Daimon Shuzō

This brewery has rigorously maintained its attention to quality with meticulous small-batch brewing, while investing in state-of-the-art machinery for polishing rice, a robot for making ginjō kōji, and other equipment to facilitate top-level production. Daimon sake is distinguished by its pure-rice flavors, and the company uses locally grown Yamada Nishiki rice. This producer is the focus of attention for its pioneering activities, including the development of overseas outlets (particularly in the United States), and the establishment of the restaurant Mukunetei—open only from Fridays to Sundays—within the brewery. *Sake on page 41.*

Hyōgo Prefecture

Nada

Slice it any way you like, it is impossible to make a list of sake-producing regions without putting Nada at the top in capital letters. This area of Hyōgo Prefecture, which includes sections of Nishinomiya and Kobe cities, has been the unchallenged leader for two hundred years, and still produces around a quarter of all the sake in Japan. Some of the giant makers of the region use the kimoto or yamahai methods of making sake and, as a result, some Nada sake has characteristic yogurt-like lactic acid notes. The dry, brusque Nada sake has often been called otoko-zake, its strong, dry lines being perceived to have a masculine character. Miyamizu (the name of the traditional brewing water of the region; see page 76) is extremely hard by Japanese standards, and this is reflected in the crisp, supple dryness of Nada sake.

BREWERS' GUILD: Tanba Tōji (Tanba Region, Hyōgo)

Although probably the most famous of all the guilds, the Tanba association has seen its membership dwindle greatly over the years. However, because of its historical dominance of the adjacent sake mecca of Nada, the few remaining active Tanba tōji still produce a quantity of sake far greater than their numbers would suggest. Their style is irrevocably identified with the full, dry sake traditionally associated with the Nada breweries.

BRAND: Hakutaka
BREWERY: Hakutaka

Because of its unalloyed, powerful taste and profundity of flavor, Hakutaka (White Hawk) sake continues to be regarded as a brand of character, despite the competition coming from the many great names of the surrounding Nada

---

酒の名前

Themes for Sake Names
④ Regional Names and Landmarks

Landmarks throughout the country lend their names to sake brands. The Japanese landmark par excellence is Mount Fuji, which has its own share of sake labels. The giant maker Shirayuki (the name of which—white snow—is said to refer to the white cap that crowns Mount Fuji all year round) has an advertising slogan that tells drinkers, "What Mount Fuji is to mountains, Shirayuki is to sake." There is a tradition of naming mountains that have an aesthetically pleasing shape such-and-such Fuji (with a regional tag), and many of these names also find their way onto sake bottles. Lots of other mountains are used as brand names, as are rivers, lakes, and other natural features, not to mention manmade landmarks such as bridges and castles.

Landmarks, Natural Features and Local Names

Izumo Fuji (Fuji of Izumo)
Dewa no Fuji (Fuji of Dewa)
Tateyama (mountain of same name)
Gassan (mountain of same name)
Shira Taki (White Waterfall; written using different characters for the word *taki*)
Nagara-gawa (river of same name)
Shimanto-gawa (river of same name)
Akita Bijin (Akita beauty)
Nanbu Bijin (Nanbu beauty)
Shirakawa Go (a village of thatched houses, that is a World Heritage Site)
Shirasagi no Shiro (White Heron Castle—Himeji Castle)

Akita Bijin

Shirakawa Go

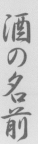

Themes for Sake Names

⑤ Local Pride, Health, and Good Fortune

One of the commonest patterns in sake names is to combine the traditional name of a region with a modestly boastful phrase. Another favorite method is to add a felicitous element.

Japanese words with which to blow your own trumpet.

Homare	誉	pride of...
Tsukasa	司	paragon of...
Nishiki	錦	literally, brocade: by extension, glory of...
Jiman	自慢	pride of...
Sakari	盛り	prime of...

Kita no Homare (Pride of the North, Hokkaido)
Oki no Homare (Pride of Oki, Shimane)
Tama Jiman (Pride of Tama, Tokyo)

Many sake brand names are chosen for associations of long life and good fortune.

Japanese words that bring luck

Kotobuki	寿	felicitations and general good luck
Chōju	長寿	long life
Kaiun	開運	impending good fortune
Fuku	福	good fortune, luck
Sachi	幸	blessings

Furō Chōju (perpetual youth and long life)
Kaiun (bearer of good fortune, page 64)
Kotobuki (general good luck)
Furō-sen (fountain of eternal youth)
Sachi-hime (princess of blessings)
Fuku no Tomo (good fortune's friend)

Oki no Homare

Furō-sen

---

district. From washing the kegs for taru-zake with sake, to ensure the best flavor, to using the finest Yamada Nishiki rice, the company takes an unstinting approach to materials and preparation, which has borne excellent results. *Sake on page 80.*

BRAND: Kamitaka
BREWERY: Eigashima Shuzō

The maker of Kamitaka (Divine Hawk) sake has a proud history dating back 320 years. Producing not only sake, but White Oak whiskey and Charmant wine (at its Yamanashi winery), this medium-sized company is a multi-faceted producer.

Its sake shows a settled flavor that is dry with a razor-sharp finish. Sweetness has been almost entirely eliminated from the equation. Anything but gaudy, Kamitaka sake, with an embedded bitterness, has the tasteful allure of niello silver, and has been delighting fans of dry sake for many years.

Kamitaka, Dai Ginjō

BRAND: Kamitaka
TYPE: Dai ginjō
BREWERY: Eigashima Shuzō

This is not a very fragrant sake, but it condenses the wealth of flavors derived from Yamada Nishiki rice into a compact form. Although seeming somewhat flat at first, the flavor is characterized by a tremendous density. It is a dai ginjō that shines at room temperature or above.

BRAND: Kenbishi
BREWERY: Kenbishi Shuzō

The Kenbishi name was already famous as one of Japan's three great sake brands during the Edo period, since when it has slaked the thirst of sake connoisseurs—including many artists and literati. When the mantle of the brewing mecca passed from Itami to Nada, this brewery followed, and continues to enjoy an excellent brand image. *Sake on page 49.*

BRAND: Tatsuriki
BREWERY: Honda Shōten

This brewery has taken pursuit of the finest rice to the limits. In line with the saying, "He who wishes to buy fine sake rice should start by buying land," the company has growing contracts with many farmers, including those of the Akitsu region around the town of Tojo, said to be the finest growing area for Yamada Nishiki rice. Apart from Yamada Nishiki and Gohyakuman-goku, the company has recently been using Omachi, Jinriki, and Yamadaho (this last the parent variety of Yamada Nishiki).

The company's products share a sense of finely woven, dense flavor that shows the characteristics of the various rice varieties to the full. *Sake on page 81.*

 BREWERS' GUILD: Tajima Tōji (Tajima Region, Hyōgo)

The Tajima brewers come from Hyōgo Prefecture, as does the Tanba union, but from the remote Tajima region in the north. Geographical circumstances dictated that men from Tajima were never as dominant in Nada as those from Tanba, and as a consequence, they were active over a very wide area, particularly in the Kansai region. (I started brewing with a veteran Tajima team in a Nara brewery.) Typical Tajima sake is full-bodied and rich in deep umami flavor.

Tokushima Prefecture

 BRAND: Naruto Tai
BREWERY: Honke Matsuura Shuzō-jō

With 60 percent of yeast starter made in the yamahai mode, the distinctive, pervasive acidity that is a characteristic of the style gives a unifying quality to the rich flavors of Naruto Tai sake. In a prefecture where sweet, light sake is the rule, Naruto Tai is a distinctive presence in the Chūgoku region. Having recently developed the talked-about Kirizukuri system (vaporizing the sake to result in a product with twenty-five percent alcohol content), and having completed construction of a new brewery in 1999, this company combines ancient and modern techniques in its pursuit of top-level brewing.

Naruto Tai, Junmai Ginjō Genshu

BRAND: Naruto Tai
TYPE: Junmai ginjō genshu
BREWERY: Honke Matsuura Shuzō-jō

A powerful individuality shows itself in the subtle character of the permeating acidity. The uniting element of rich, satisfying flavor is the trademark of the Tajima brewers' guild. This brewery excels in the deep flavor perspectives of the kimoto and yamahai school: like many excellent Naruto Tai sakes, this is first-rate warmed—which is also a common feature of Tajima tōji creations.

Kagawa Prefecture

 BRAND: Ayakiku
BREWERY: Ayakiku Shuzō

Reflecting on the meaning of the term ji-zake led this brewery to focus on the local rice strain, Oseto. Since Oseto is not a true brewer's rice, Ayakiku took on a tall order by choosing to use it, even to make sake for entry in the National Assessment for New Sake. Their thirteen-year run of Gold Medals in spite of this handicap is a monumental achievement. At the time of writing, this record of success (carried out within the tenure of master brewer Hiroaki Kunishige) is unbroken.

Kōchi Prefecture

With around twenty producers, the region of Kōchi is not in the top division in terms of production volume. On the consumption side, however, the people of Tosa (the traditional name for the region) are big leaguers. The typical style of the sake is an easy-drinking dry to facilitate large-scale consumption. Compared to the crystalline style of dry Niigata sake (page 65), for example, the Tosa brews tend to have a slightly grainier, rounder feel. In the last few years, a number of products brewed using deep-sea water have brought renewed attention to the region. Ginjō brewing in the region has received a boost from the high-octane fragrances of the locally developed CEL (pronounced cell) Yeast.

Okayama Prefecture

 BRAND: Kamo Midori, Chikurin
BREWERY: Marumoto Shuzō

Calling itself an agricultural storehouse, this company brews using Yamada Nishiki grown in its own rice fields. The brewery buildings, which lie in the gentle slopes of rice paddies, have been designated a Cultural Asset. The company brews in a style rich in pure flavor, with a blossoming umami. Its main brand names are Kamo Midori and Chikurin. As well as its sparkling sake (designed to bring non-sake fans into the fold), it uses the White Peach Yeast developed by Okayama Prefecture, and produces a liqueur using the peaches for which the region is well known. *Sake on page 51.*

Shimane Prefecture

 BRAND: Rihaku (also Wandering Poet)
BREWERY: Rihaku Shuzō

The lavish approach of this brewery sees local brewers' rice used even for non-premium products. The rich, full-bodied style of Rihaku sake is typical of its home region, and realized thanks to the fine quality of the raw materials used. As Wandering Poet, this is a popular import in the United States.

Rihaku, Junmai Ginjō, Chōtokusen

 BRAND: Rihaku (also Wandering Poet)
TYPE: Junmai ginjō
BREWERY: Rihaku Shuzō

Within a plump complex of taste and aroma, a scent of nuts with a sweet impression drifts around the mouth. The softness on the tongue belies the depth of flavor, making this a sake that performs well whether lightly chilled or warmed.

◄ The kōji is parceled into 3.3-pound (1.5-kilogram) lots in wooden trays on day two of the classical *futa* method (see page 86).

Hiroshima Prefecture

BRAND: Fukuchō
BREWERY: Imada Shuzō

Once upon a time, mineral-poor soft water with its subdued fermentation characteristics was held to be difficult water for brewing. Hiroshima is said to be the pioneer that overcame this, spawning the ginjō genre by using low-temperature fermentation to give finely textured sake. This company continues the tradition today, paying close attention to a smooth flow of flavor in brewing its rounded sake.

The master brewer is none other than the owner's daughter, Miho Imada, and the company is also well known as one of the few breweries to have a female tōji.

Fukuchō Saya, Ginjō

BRAND: Fukuchō
TYPE: Ginjō
BREWERY: Imada Shuzō

With a smooth texture on the tongue, this is a sake with a light touch that has refreshing scents reminiscent of strawberry and pear drifting through the mouth. The vivid aromatics give a well-modulated feeling to the whole, and the gorgeous fragrance makes a lingering impression in the aftertaste.

BRAND: Hanahato
BREWERY: Enoki Shuzō

Although the tōji here is still in his thirties, he is a master at brewing with the newly developed Hiroshima rice Senbon Nishiki, and his work has received honors in the various industry contests. Hanahato can certainly be considered a rising star in the firmament of the brewers' heaven that is Hiroshima. *Sake on page 50.*

BRAND: Kamotsuru
BREWERY: Kamotsuru Shuzō

A smooth texture, characteristic of the products of soft-water brewing, combined with a full aroma and flavor, is the signature of this brewery, long a leader of the Hiroshima school of brewing. Beginning with its high placings in the national sake contest late in the Meiji (1868–1912) period, and its pioneering ginjō brewing (which is said to have originated in Hiroshima), it is not too much to say that the history of this brewery and the history of the Hiroshima school are one and the same. Its *Dai Ginjō Gold Kamotsuru* (see next entry) and various other products retain the high status they have long enjoyed during the traditional seasons for formal gift-giving.

▶ The characteristics of a water source are a key element defining the style of the sake from a particular brewery.

宮水
The Discovery of Miyamizu

The most famous brewing water in Japan is that found in Nada, Hyōgo Prefecture. The Nada region has been the most prolific sake-producing area since Miyamizu water (*mizu* means water, and *miya* is derived from the place name Nishinomiya) was discovered a little over 160 years ago. The story of its discovery is one of the sake world's most famous.

The hero of the tale is one Tazaemon Yamamura, the owner of the brewing concern known today as Sakura Masamune. He owned breweries in two locations a few miles apart, and was perplexed by the fact that the sake from the Nishinomiya brewery was always better.

He set out to discover what factor was responsible for the difference. He used the same rice, and even went as far as to exchange all the brewing equipment. Even switching brewers made no difference (to the great relief of the tōji from the other brewery, one imagines).

When he undertook the costly business of transporting water by cart from Nishinomiya, at last the mystery was solved. The secret was in the water. Once the magical properties of Miyamizu had been discovered, all the Nada breweries began using it, as they do today. Nada became a benchmark for the industry, and brewers flocked to the area specifically to gain access to the mystique—and the practical benefits—of the water.

Shrine to the divinity of the brewing water at Ozawa Shuzō (page 63). Sake brewing is intimately involved with Shinto beliefs, and all breweries have shrines or altars for the sake divinity. The characters on the stone basin read "God of the Sake Spring."

Dai Ginjō, Gold Kamotsuru

BRAND: Kamotsuru
TYPE: Dai ginjō
BREWERY: Kamotsuru Shuzō

This is a dai ginjō that can be enjoyed over a wide temperature range, both chilled and warmed. Following the faint top fragrance, an expansive flavor unfolds on the tongue. The profound structure and indescribable umami make it easy to see why this sake is found at first-class restaurants around the country.

Yamaguchi Prefecture

BRAND: Dassai
BREWERY: Asahi Shuzō

The sake made by Asahi Shuzō is characterized by a lively fragrance and refreshing flavor that have given it increasing popularity in recent years. All products are junmai ginjō class, and are distinguished by the rice polishing ratio.

The name Dassai is written with characters that mean otter festival. Although the character for otter (獺) occurs in the name of the remote region where the brewery is located, the brand name refers to the otter's habit of laying out the fish it has caught on the riverbank like stalls at a festival. The company also makes Otter Fest Beer. *Sake on page 42.*

BRAND: Gokyō
BREWERY: Sakai Shuzō

The brand name (literally meaning five bridges) commemorates the five spans of the local landmark, the Kintaikyō Bridge. All the brewery's products show a lingering balance of the so-called five flavors (sweetness, dryness, acidity, bitterness, and astringency). This style is a model of the sake of western Japan. *Sake on page 44.*

Saga Prefecture

The southern island of Kyūshū is famous for shōchū spirit rather than sake, but, with the single exception of Kagoshima, every prefecture in Kyūshū has its share of sake breweries. Saga has thirty or so. In an age where dry sake is preferred, this prefecture produces a soft, sweet style, very gentle on the palate. It is a chicken-and-egg conundrum, but it is interesting to contemplate whether the high proportion of the local brews consumed within the prefecture is responsible for the distinctive style, or vice versa.

BRAND: Mado no Ume
BREWERY: Mado no Ume Shuzō

Founded some 320 years ago, this is one of the southern island of Kyūshū's most venerable breweries. Despite being in Saga, where sweet sake is mainstream, this brewery is skilled in producing a strong-boned, dry style of sake. *Sake on page 39.*

chapter Four

The Brewer's Craft

Sake makes an appearance not only at flower-viewing and moon-viewing parties, but also at auspicious occasions such as weddings, where gifts are adorned with sculpted *mizuhiki* cords (like those in a crane motif shown here). Auspicious colors and themes are also prevalent on sake labels and packaging.

There are ten thousand schools of brewing.
(*Sake-zukuri banryū*)

—Sake industry saying

All sake brewers are basically doing the same thing: changing starch (the raw material of rice) into sugar, which is then converted to alcohol using yeast. Despite this common ground, details of brewing practices vary tremendously. The following discussion covers the textbook version of the classical brewing method. In real life, every single brewery has its own textbook—often several different textbooks for different products.

The main stages of brewing are as follows.

Sugidama. Made of the needles of the Japanese cedar (*sugi*) woven into a bamboo lattice, this furry sphere was the mark of sake brewery in a pre-literate age.

STAGE 1: THE TREATMENT OF RAW MATERIALS
The rice is polished to remove the brown outer part, then washed and soaked in water before being steamed.

STAGE 2: THE PRODUCTION OF *KŌJI*
A peculiar but very handy mold is grown on steamed rice. It converts the starch of the rice grains into fermentable sugars.

STAGE 3: THE PRODUCTION OF THE YEAST STARTER (*SHUBO* OR *MOTO*)
Pure sake yeast cultures are propagated in a small starter batch.

STAGE 4: THE PREPARATION AND FERMENTATION OF THE MAIN MASH (*MOROMI*)
Rice, finished kōji, and water are added to the yeast starter, and the main fermentation begins.

STAGE 5: PRESSING (FORMALLY *JŌSŌ*; CONVERSATIONALLY, *SHIBORI*)
The fermenting mash is pressed to separate the sake from the solids.

STAGE 6: AFTER-PRESSING TREATMENT, STORAGE, AND SHIPPING
The new sake is filtered and pasteurized before aging. It is usually refiltered, diluted, and pasteurized before bottling and sale.

THE RAW MATERIALS

The first task facing the aspiring brewer is to ensure a supply of rice and water, often called the mother and father of sake.

Water

Sake is 80 percent water, and the quality of that water has an enormous influence on the final product. Great brewing centers grew up near sources of excellent water.

Simply put, there is good water and bad water. Some minerals are good news for fermentation, but, since they are far more abundant in rice than in water, it is more important for brewing water to be low in contaminants than rich in desirable elements. The worst news you could have about your brewing water is that it is iron-heavy. Iron is very bad for the flavor and aroma of sake. Although it is possible to filter out iron and other nasties, it is an expensive process, so a copious supply of good water is a financial blessing for a brewery. Association with a famous water source or spring is a valuable asset in this image-laden business.

Hard water, or water that is mineral-heavy, makes for a strong, vigorous fermentation. This means breweries using hard water generally have a shorter fermentation time, and the resulting sake will incline to dryness and a sharper, crisper flavor profile. Soft-water brewing sees a longer fermentation period, since the activity of the yeast is more subdued. The resulting sake tends to sweetness, and will be fuller and softer on the palate than its hard-water cousins.

Kinmatsu Hakutaka, Tokubetsu Junmai

BRAND: Hakutaka
TYPE: Tokubetsu junmai
BREWERY: Hakutaka, in Hyōgo Prefecture

With a wealth of flavor elements—bitterness, sweetness—combining around an axis of tangy acidity to give breadth, this is a solid, beefy junmai with plenty of body in the true Nada tradition. For details about Nada's legendary brewing water, see page 77.

Rice

The ancestors of the fat-grained Japonica rice strains grown in Japan today are thought to have arrived from continental Asia with the techniques of wet-rice (paddy-field) agriculture a little over two thousand years ago. Anthropologists believe that the intense communal cooperation necessary for this form of agriculture was a factor in developing the Japanese tendency to group-oriented behavior. Considering that rice plays a central role in Shinto religious ritual, and that it was long used for paying taxes, it has a much more important role in Japanese life and thought than that of a simple foodstuff.

Rice in Brewing

Originally, brewing made use of whatever rice happened to be grown locally. In time, though, brewers found certain strains to be particularly suited to sake mak-

Techniques, Ancient and Modern
Part 1: Rice Polishing

Japanese households used to polish their table rice by putting it in a big sake bottle, and ramming a wooden stick through it again and again. A large-scale version of this mortar-and-pestle way of applying friction to the grains was also used in days past by brewers. Known as *ashifumi seimai*, polishing by stomping, it involved the raising of a long wooden beam like a seesaw, simply by standing on one end of it. When the worker stepped off, the weighted end would drop down into the receptacle of rice currently being polished. Repeat as necessary. Polishing took a day and a night.

This first stage of brewing was also the first to be mechanized. It was the pioneering brewers of Nada who did this, in the late eighteenth century. Nada lies between the mountains and the coast of Hyōgo Prefecture. There are several rivers that come barreling down the hillsides, and the breweries harnessed them to waterwheels. Apart from the savings in time and labor costs, it became possible to polish the rice further than before. Initially, about ten percent had been the limit, but it became possible to polish away almost a third of the kernel. The highly polished rice absorbed water better, which made it possible to make more sake from the same quantity of rice. The clean flavor of the resulting sake found a delighted public.

But the development of the technology had just begun. From manpower to waterpower was the first step, followed by the move to steam, and, finally, electric generators. The latest generation of machines is also computer-controlled, which means that polishing can be carried out twenty-four hours a day without the need to have a bleary eyed worker on the graveyard shift.

Modern rice-polishing machinery is designed so that the rice flows down over rotating millstones arranged on a vertical axis. This vertical layout made it possible to polish the rice further without the grains heating up too much—an insuperable problem with horizontal machines. As a result, it became practical to polish rice to the high levels needed to make ginjō sake, a prosaic technical development that has given the industry its most glamorous star.

Part 2:
Washing Rice in the Old Days

The first tōji I worked for, Tetsuo Ishihara, told me a lot of stories about his days as an apprentice brewer in his teens, when washing rice was one of the hardest jobs. It was not so much a question of *hand* washing as washing by leg power. The system was to put the rice in a wooden tub of water, into which the kurabito climbed—with bare feet. The rice was washed by swishing it around in a circular motion with the feet, each batch being washed by a fixed number of movements. This task was carried out at the beginning of the day (which in a traditional sake brewery meant well before dawn), and took most of the freezing winter morning.

Rising Stars and Returning Heroes

Specific regions have developed a number of new varieties in recent years. A few examples are Ginginga (from Iwate Prefecture), Dewa sansan (from Yamagata Prefecture) and Ginnoyume (from Kōchi on the island of Shikoku).

These three are new arrivals on the stage, but another feature of recent decades has been the revival of dormant varieties. A strain will go out of production because it is hard to grow or tricky to handle in brewing. Later, some enterprising soul will wangle a few grains from the collections of agricultural research organizations or universities, and go about giving the variety in question a new lease of life. The most famous example is the Kame no O strain, the comeback of which (orchestrated by Kusumi Shuzō in Niigata Prefecture) was fictionalized and made famous in the comic book *Natsuko no Sake*.

ing. These had especially large grains and an opaque white center (*shinpaku*). Although plenty of tasty sake is still made from varieties of table rice (for eating), the finest sake is held to be that made from the big-grained brewers' rice.

Brewers' rice tends to be long in the stalk and vulnerable to the typhoons that sweep disastrously across the country every year during the growing season. It is harder work for farmers, lower yielding than table-rice varieties, and consequently more expensive.

Individual Rice Varieties

Dozens of rice varieties are used in sake brewing, but their influence on the final flavor is not as all-pervasive as is true of the various strains of grape used in wine making. If you are a varietally minded wine drinker, you will need to change mental gears in this respect. Here are a few of the commoner strains and their characteristics.

Yamada Nishiki—A survey of rice varieties used in brewing necessarily begins with Yamada Nishiki. Though produced less widely (and in slightly smaller quantity) than Gohyakuman-goku (see below), it really is number one in every other sense.

So, where did this titan originate? Registered way back in 1936 in Hyōgo Prefecture, it is by far the most successful of the hybrid strains developed in the twentieth century. The caché of the name has led other regions and even individual breweries to try their hands at growing Yamada Nishiki. However, it is not grown in the far north, where climatic conditions are unsuitable, and it never performs as well away from home.

Brewers find it a very biddable rice; it is easier to get things right with Yamada Nishiki. The increasing popularity of high-grade ginjō sake in recent years has only confirmed its preeminence, as brewers find it gives a fruity, well-bred style and a charismatic blossoming of flavor to the finished product. Yamada Nishiki sake also ages elegantly.

Tatsuriki, Dai Ginjō, Kome no Sasayaki

BRAND: Tatsuriki
TYPE: Dai Ginjō
BREWERY: Honda Shōten, in Hyōgo Prefecture

This shows depth of ample flavor, with sake's five tastes (sweet, dry, sour, bitter, and astringent) expressed to the full. The power of the rush of rich, mellow flavor really shows why Yamada Nishiki is so often described as the king of sake rice.

Omachi—If Yamada Nishiki is the Windows of sake rice, Omachi is surely the only contender of sufficient charisma to qualify as a candidate for Macintosh.

Where Omachi wins hands down over Yamada is in the ripping yarn category. Unlike Yamada, which was deliberately bred by agriculturalists, Omachi is an act of God, a natural variation discovered in Okayama Prefecture more than a century ago. Other comparably venerable strains are grown, but all the others passed out of production at one time or other, to be resurrected from a few grains preserved in the archives of research institutes. Omachi is the only rice variety to have been in continuous cultivation for so long. Even so, when the sake industry was in its most monolithic period in the 1960s and 1970s, the number of acres (hectares) under cultivation dropped right down to single figures. Since then, however, it has been increasingly in demand as brewers look to find fine rice that will give their sake distinction.

Okayama Prefecture is still the unchallenged center of production, though a little is grown in neighboring Hiroshima. Compared to the three most widely produced varieties, Omachi is really still a minor strain in terms of volume. Even now, it is sometimes called *maboroshi no sakamai* (*sakamai* translates as sake rice; *maboroshi*—a dream, if not a mirage—is the Japanese marketing person's favorite word for anything rare and sought-after). The reason for this is that it is extremely hard work to grow. Yamada Nishiki's height of over one meter is often compared to that of table-rice strains (usually between 28 and 35 inches/70 and 90 centimeters) to stress the trials faced by producers of brewers' rice. Yet Omachi grows to a towering 47 inches/120 centimeters, and requires late harvesting into the bargain.

For the brewer's purposes, the very large grain size is a welcome attribute on the positive side. However, Omachi is said to be the softest of all brewer's rice strains. Unlike Yamada Nishiki, which seems happy to do all the right things, it is very difficult to handle. Mention of Omachi will cause many a brewer to shake his head mournfully, muttering, *"Ano kome wa muzukashii"* ("It's a tricky one, that rice").

In the hands of a brewer who is both skilled and experienced in the use of the strain, however, Omachi can give a sake the depth, fullness, and limpidity of Yamada Nishiki brews, with an extra herbaceous dimension of wild flowers or even dried herbs, characteristics that take on fascinating complexities during aging.

Ume no Yado, Bizen Omachi, Junmai Dai Ginjō

BRAND: Ume no Yado
TYPE: Junmai dai ginjō
BREWERY: Ume no Yado, in Nara Prefecture

With fruity fragrances of melon and peach, acidity works subtly in the balance to give both breadth and crispness of flavor. Sake made with Omachi rice tends to have a fat acidity concealed behind the sweet rice flavor, and this characteristic finds full expression here.

Miyama Nishiki—Miyama Nishiki was developed in Nagano Prefecture, from a strain previously made for brewing called Takane Nishiki. This proved to be a little too small in the grain for brewers to really take to, and the agricultural boffins zapped it until they got a mutant offspring with a bigger grain and a higher incidence of *shinpaku* (white heart). As it approaches its thirtieth birthday, it has proved itself to be a highly regarded brewing rice. It is hardy and grows well in areas too cold for Yamada Nishiki, and so is widely produced in Nagano and more northerly prefectures. It gives an elegant, fine-lined feel to sake.

▶ Preparing to hoist the steamed rice (see page 84).

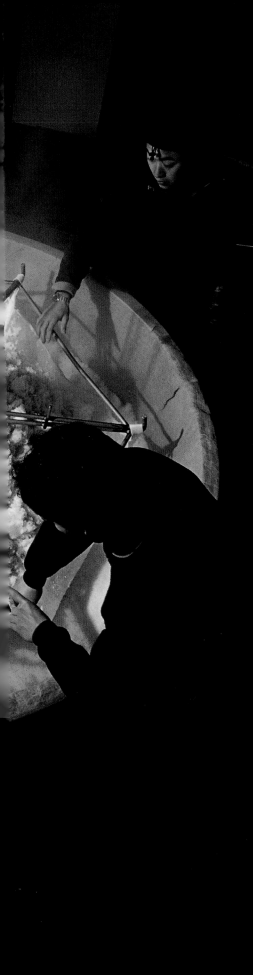

Gohyakuman-goku—In terms of production quantity, this is the top sake rice strain. It has been around for almost fifty years, and might have arrived a little earlier if World War II had not interrupted the efforts of the Niigata Agricultural Research Institute. The name, meaning five million *koku*, was chosen to celebrate Niigata Prefecture farmers' total rice production reaching the five-million-*koku* (750,000-ton) mark. Sake made from Gohyakuman-goku rice tends to be lightish in flavor, without the lively elastic quality for which Yamada Nishiki is prized. Colleagues have told me that it is well suited to the making of machine-made kōji.

Ippongi Junmaishu

BRAND: Ippongi
TYPE: Junmai
BREWERY: Ippongi Kubo Honten, in Fukui Prefecture

It is said that brewing with Gohyakuman-goku rice produces sake with less flavor than Yamada Nishiki. In this case, there is a somewhat flat impression, but the brewer succeeds in presenting a subtle expanse of flavor by melting sour and bitter notes into an understated whole. The very settled structure of this sake makes it a great companion for food, and it can be enjoyed at room temperature or lightly warmed.

Junmai Dai Ginjō, Kame no O

BRAND: Kiyoizumi
TYPE: Junmai Dai Ginjō
BREWERY: Kusumi Shuzō, in Niigata Prefecture

This sake gives a soft impression on the palate, with an enveloping, refreshing fragrance of strawberry and peach. A sprightly acidity makes itself felt within the quiet overall impression, creating a pleasant fresh sensation. This is a delicate, limpid dai ginjō in the true mold of the sake from the north.

YK35

For many years, the accepted formula for brewing prize-winning sake was YK35. Y stands for Yamada Nishiki; K represents Association Yeast No. 9 (which originated in Kumamoto Prefecture), and 35 is the percentage representing the recommended rice-polishing ratio.

In the last two decades, new yeast strains have ended the era of dominance by Yeast No. 9 (though it remains immensely important as a commercial ginjô yeast), but there is, at the time of writing, absolutely no serious challenger for the throne of Yamada Nishiki.

Its supremacy was recently tacitly reaffirmed at the highest levels when the Brewing Research Center in Hiroshima reorganized the criteria for entering sake in its prestigious annual National Assessment for New Sake. Previously, there had been no restrictions on the kind of rice used for brewing. As of 2001, however, the hopeful brewer must enter his or her baby in one of two sections. Section Two is for sake made from Yamada Nishiki. Section One is for All Other Strains—but includes less than ten percent of all entries.

THE PROCESS OF SAKE BREWING

Polishing Rice

The first step in brewing is the polishing of the rice, or *seimai*. The outer portion is ground away, leaving the starchy center of the grain for use in brewing (see photographs on page 35). It is the mirror image of a flourmill, because the powder is a waste product as far as brewing is concerned. A purely mechanical process, it lacks the sense of microbial mystery of later stages. Even so, this first step is so important that, in days past, there was a seimai tōji as well as the tōji brew master.

The brown part of the rice grain is high in fats, proteins, and other nutrients—which is good news for a healthy diet, but not for the brewer. Polishing removes minerals and proteins, leaving a higher ratio of pure starch to be converted to sake. The further the rice is polished, the clearer and cleaner will be the taste of the resulting sake. Too much nutrition for the yeast makes fermentation hard to control, and the outer portion of the grain causes musty smells, which have found ever fewer admirers over the centuries.

The machinery itself works by dropping a flow of rice over rotating millstones. The rice powder is sucked out by a kind of giant vacuum cleaner; the whole grains drop to the bottom of the machine before being carried to the top to begin the cycle again. The rice circulates in the machine until it has been polished to the target size.

Cooling-Off Period

The size of the rice grains is reduced by friction in the polishing process. This creates heat, which means that the more the rice is polished, the lower the moisture content of the grains. If the rice is washed immediately, the desiccated grains absorb water at such a rate that they may crack from the sudden shock. Time for the rice to reabsorb moisture from the air is a luxury for which any brewer wishes—especially when making ginjō sake. This period is called *karashi*.

Washing the Rice

After polishing is finished, the brewer thoroughly washes off rice powder that remains on the surface of the rice grains, since it would cause problems later on.

The simplest system for washing rice involves the pumping of the rice with water through a suitable length of piping. The brewer can kill two birds with one stone by transporting the rice and washing it at the same time. Most of the rice powder has been washed off by the time the journey through the pipe has ended, by which time the water will be cloudy (just as it is after table rice has been washed at home). At the end of the journey, there is a final shower of clean water to wash away the milky water with its load of rice powder.

Washing using one of a variety of machines is the rule in modern brewing, but many brewers still insist on hand washing the rice to be used in making the highest grades of sake. Generally, hand washing consists of swooshing the rice around a basket placed in a shallow vat of water. Recent years have also seen the increasing use of a variety of machines designed to wash rice gently in small lots—attempts to mechanize hand washing. These vary from simple devices to circulate

rice and water mechanically in a small tub, to elaborate robotic gadgets. After washing, the rice is rinsed once again to sluice off the cloudy water.

Steeping

The rice used in brewing is soaked in water to make it possible to steam through to the heart of the grains.

The soaking is done after washing. The time varies according to the temperature of the water, the variety and quality of rice, the grade of polish, and the water content of the grain. Once soaking is finished, the rice is lifted out of the water and drained, then left overnight until the next stage.

STEEPING TIMES AND WHY THEY VARY. Rice polished to only about 70 percent of its original size absorbs all the water it can in an hour or thereabouts. Life is not so simple when making Premium grade sakes, however. Brewer's rice strains are more absorbent than table-rice varieties, and the low moisture content of the highly polished rice used in making high-grade sake means that they soak up water at a fearsome rate. In extreme cases, the soaking period may last only a few minutes, with an error of seconds meaning no end of grief in the weeks that must pass before the batch in question is finished.

The nerve-wracking system of removing the rice from the water at the right point to stop further absorption is called *gentei kyūsui* (limited water absorption). The alternative is to adjust the water content of the grain before washing so that it cannot absorb more than the desired level of moisture. This *chōshitsu* system is labor-intensive, however, and many brewers still wash rice with a stopwatch and a furrowed brow.

Steaming
See photographs on pages 82 and 86.

Essentially, sake is made by dissolving rice; steaming makes this possible. Just as rice is cooked to change the rigid starch of the raw grain into fluffy, edible form, so the brewer alters the structure of the starch by steaming. All the rice used in classical brewing is steamed, though some breweries use a new technology to bypass this step.

The traditional steamer used in sake breweries is a pot called a

Sake Brewer's Blues

Sake brewing used to entail a lot of repetitive heavy labor, often carried out at highly unsociable hours. One palliative to such tasks was a variety of task-specific songs that were sung to while away the time and help stave off weariness during the small hours, with lyrics expressing the hardships of the brewer's life in the manner of spirituals or the blues. They also helped timekeeping in repetitious work. The master brewer adjusted the degree of washing (or the various other tasks), by stipulating the number of times the song was to be sung during the process at hand.

Guard the Rice—At Any Cost

Sake brewing at every stage is all about temperature control, so the task of transporting the rice in the cold winter air allows little room for error—it has to arrive at its destination at the right temperature. All other business stops until this has finished. A veteran colleague of mine told me how, in his youth, a section of a staircase gave way under him while he was carrying steamed rice to the kōji culture room. Lying injured on his back, unable to move, he watched helplessly as his colleagues stepped over him as they carried their loads of rice into the culture room. It was only when all the rice had been safely delivered that they stopped to help him.

koshiki. This system limits batch size, and lends itself to smaller scale, traditional brewing styles. Large-scale brewing usually uses a conveyor-belt apparatus.

Rice is steamed a total of eight times in the production of a single batch of sake, and the steamed rice is used at different temperatures for different stages. It is usually cooled on a large mesh conveyor with fans attached, though it may be spread out and cooled naturally in some stages in hand brewing. The rice cools as it moves along the conveyor belt, and is parceled out to its various destinations when it falls off the end. Fully mechanized breweries transport all the rice with air blowers that whiz it through pipes to where it is needed. Some small and traditional breweries still carry the rice by hand, wheelbarrow, or other less-automated means. *See the endpapers for more information.*

STAGE 2 *Kōji*

About a fifth of all the rice used is taken to a humid room, which is kept heated to around 86° F (30° C), in order to be made into kōji, which takes more than two days per batch. If you imagine a bowl of rice (or a sandwich, for that matter) left for two days in a hot, sweaty environment, you might think that it would become pretty moldy. And that is precisely what happens. Kōji is a mold. It is not a nasty, smelly mildewy mold, though, but a fragrant, hygienic-looking white one. If you have eaten blue cheese (also a product of mold cultures) and lived to tell the tale, you will find kōji very easy on the eye.

Kōji creates a supply of glucose as nutrition for yeast, which in turn transforms the sugar into alcohol. From the drinker's point of view, it is also a primary source of the characteristic aromas and flavors that make drinking sake fun.

The Making of *Kōji*

The brewer begins by carrying the steamed rice into the culture room where it is spread out in a thin layer. When the rice has cooled to a little over 86° F (30° C), spores of the mold (proper name Aspergillus

▶ Sluicing cloudy water from rice after washing. The device pictured is in use at the Doi Shuzō brewery (page 64).

Steam escapes through a canvas cover during the steaming of the rice.

oryzae) are shaken over it like a fine dust, then kneaded evenly into the grains. On day one, the brewer aims to prevent the rice from drying and cooling, so it is wrapped in cloths in one big bundle. About twelve hours later, workers break the heap down and mix it around to even out temperature and moisture content—the two key elements influencing the growth pattern of the mold. Then the batch is swaddled in cloths again overnight.

The following morning, white flecks are visible on the surface of the grain where the spores have started their growth. The mold gives off heat as it grows, so the batch is broken into small lots to keep temperature and moisture content under close control. The classical method sees the rice divided and placed on small wooden trays called *futa* (about 3.3 pounds/1.5 kilograms per tray; see photograph on page 74). A variant of this uses boxes that hold between 22 and 33 pounds/10 and 15 kilograms). The rice is heaped in the middle to begin with, then gradually spread out to disperse the heat that is given off as the mold grows. Usually, workers will mix the contents of the boxes twice before the batch is finished—once around twelve hours after the original division, and then four hours later. (When the smaller futa are being used, they are kept in stacks, and they must also be rotated within the stack: the top one to the bottom, left to right, and so on) to keep the temperature even throughout the pile.) The temperature of the kōji finally reaches some 110° to 113° F (43° to 45° C). On day three, the growth of the mold is stopped by taking it out of the

humid culture room to cool down. The finished kōji is hard, white, and not at all sticky—quite unlike the steamed rice with which it was made. It has a smell rather like roast chestnuts, and when chewed, is slightly sweet. It is this sweetness that will be food for the yeast during fermentation.

This is the traditional method of making kōji by hand. Though many breweries still make kōji in this fashion, nowadays a great deal of it is made by machine, varying from robots that essentially reproduce the conditions of the traditional system (right down to the wooden boxes), to enormous two-story apparatuses.

STAGE 3 The Yeast Starter

Yeast is an organism that changes sugar into alcohol, but sake yeast is different than that used to make wine or beer. All the many strains of sake yeast handle differently to give varying nuances to the finished sake.

Since the Middle Ages, Japanese brewers have devoted a separate stage of brewing to the propagation of pure and lively sake yeast. This is the yeast starter or seed mash, and is known as shubo (literally sake mother), or *moto*. Shubo is loaded with sake yeast molecules (about four hundred million of the little guys in a single drop of liquid), and very sour. The sourness is a key point, since high levels of acidity inhibit the growth of troublemaking bacteria. Healthy starter smells fantastic, and the aromatic signature of the end product sake is here in concentrated form.

There are two basic styles in which the yeast starter is produced. The quick-fermenting method (*sokujō*) is the standard in modern brewing.

Eikō Fuji, Ginjō Shōnai-Homare

SAKE

BRAND: Shōnai-Homare
TYPE: Ginjō
BREWERY: Fuji Shuzō, in Yamagata Prefecture

The soft impression on the palate is complemented by rich, mellow umami, all wreathed in refreshing melon- and apple-like aromatics. The aftertaste is also fluid and smooth: the lines of this graceful sake recall the smooth skyline of the slopes of Mount Fuji for which the company is named. The backbone of its style is Association Yeast No. 10, which gives delicate sake with low levels of acidity.

The Quick-Fermenting Method

Kōji is mixed with water and yeast, and the brewer adds lactic acid to acidify the mash. This prevents the growth of unwanted bacteria and, to a lesser extent, wild yeasts. Steamed rice is added a couple of hours later. The temperature of the rice is adjusted so that the final temperature of the mix is about 68° F (20° C). After a few hours, the rice has soaked up all the available moisture, and the surface of the mash swells into a moist dome leaving no liquid visible.

For the next couple of days, the temperature is lowered to below 50° F (10° C). This has the effect of inhibiting the growth of the yeast, while enzymes from the kōji work, making the thick mash softer and looser, and, most importantly, sweeter.

Breaking up clumps on the evening of day one in the culture room: one of the more physical tasks when making kōji.

To help this process along, a technique called *kumikake* may be used, whereby a cylinder with narrow slots at the base is forced through to the bottom of the mash, after which the rice inside the cylinder is scooped out, enabling liquid to seep up in through the slots from the rice outside. The cylindrical hollow soon fills with sour and, increasingly, sweet liquid. The kōji enzymes dissolve into the liquid, which the brewer ladles onto the surface of the mash at regular intervals. (There are also Heath-Robinson machines that perform this task and look like a mad scientist's attempt at making a tin octopus.)

After two or three days, the mash is much sweeter, and the brewer starts to raise the temperature again. (This is done by placing containers of hot water in the tank, positioning small electric heaters underneath the tank, or using a combination of both methods.) Only the portion of the mash directly in contact is affected, reaching about 123° F (55° C), the ideal temperature for sugar-producing enzymes. The initial aim is to raise sugar content before the yeast gets up a full head of steam, so the mash is cooled again overnight.

After a few days of this, the yeast begins to work as the temperature rises, and bubbles of gas caused by fermentation rise to the surface of the mash. Once the temperature rises above 60° F (15° C), the heat of the fermentation becomes self-sustaining, and the mash begins to seethe with movement as the yeast gets up a full head of steam. Foam rises above the surface as the process moves into its most vigorous stage. All the while, the action of the enzymes from the kōji is gradually liquefying the mash, which becomes progressively more fluid. By this point, the sweetness of the mix has peaked, as sugars are consumed by the yeast and acidity has increased still further. The end result is a sweet-and-sour mash containing a lively culture of dense pure-sake yeast. The density of sake yeast shuts out unreliable wild yeasts, and the high acidity inhibits the growth of unwelcome bacteria. From the drinker's point of view, the most significant feature is the fabulous fruity aroma, which proclaims the presence of healthy sake yeast in ample quantity, and promises a fine fragrance in the final sake.

If the level of alcohol rises much above 12 percent, some of the yeast begins to weaken, so the brewer reduces the temperature to below 50° F (10° C) to inhibit the production of alcohol. (In days past, the brewers managed this by physically dividing the mash into shallow vats. The Japanese verb for divide, *wakeru*, gives its name to this process still, even though modern brewers no longer physically split the mash.) The period between the cooling off of the starter and its use in the next stage of brewing is called *karashi*. A Darwinian feature of this period (usually a matter of a few days) is that the less-robust yeast dies off, leaving only the liveliest specimens to carry on the main fermentation.

Living Traditions: The *Kimoto* School and *Yamahai*

For centuries, the kimoto school's system of making the yeast starter was the standard, but was largely replaced in the twentieth-century mainstream by the quick-fermenting method. The kimoto school represents a superb system to propagate a pure, single target organism—namely sake yeast. What is so remarkable is that this high-level biotechnology was perfected in an era before its proponents even suspected the existence of yeast and the other microscopic cast members.

According to the kimoto way, the brewer mixes water and kōji as would be done according to modern methods, but leaves out the key items, lactic acid and the star of the show, yeast.

Steamed rice is added, but the brewer keeps the temperature much lower (no higher than 50° F/10° C). Mashing is carried out in several shallow tubs called *hangiri* according to the kimoto system, or in a single tank when using the revised yamahai technique.

The next stage is what distinguishes the original kimoto from the yamahai method. A few hours after mashing, the contents of the tubs are mixed lightly. Next, the mix is ground with bulbous wooden paddles. This task of *motosuri* (also called *yamaoroshi*) is carried out three times according to the kimoto technique, but is omitted entirely when following yamahai principles. (The word yamahai is a contraction of *yama-oroshi haishi moto*, which means moto-without-grinding-the-moto.)

Low temperatures are maintained for the next few days. Even so, the kōji enzymes do their work, albeit very slowly, and the stiff mash becomes gradually sweeter and softer. After a few days, the brewer begins the daily process of inserting containers of hot water to increase the quantity of sugar in the mash.

Over a period of some two weeks, the brewer gradually raises the temperature in a two-steps-forward, one-step-back pattern, during which time the activity of a series of microorganisms inhibits the growth of bacteria and wild yeasts. First on the scene are nitrate-reducing bacteria from the water. These produce toxic nitrous acid, killing wild yeasts. Next come lactic acid bacteria, which ferment to create lactic acid, reflected in the appearance of sour flavors in the ever sweeter mash. The resulting acidity polishes off the bacteria that produced the nitrous acid.

Now, lactic acid bacteria are normally one of the brewer's greatest fears, since they can spoil a batch of sake by turning it impossibly sour. In the modern methods of sake making, their growth is prevented by making the mash highly acidic at the outset. It is the peculiar characteristic of the kimoto school that the brewer deliberately cultivates his arch-enemy, relying on the fact that the lactic acid bacteria die when the acidity of the mash reaches a certain level. That said, errors of handling that disrupt the timing of this progression can spell disaster. But if all has gone well, the brewer has an acidic, sugar-dense base in which sake yeast can grow.

In premodern brewing, the brewer relied on airborne yeasts in the brewery to seed themselves; nowadays, the brewer adds pure yeast cultures. (A batch of quick-fermenting starter begun on the same day would be ready for use by now, about two weeks after mashing.) From this point on, life is relatively simple, and the brewer can raise the temperature safely and watch the yeast do its frothy stuff.

STAGE 4 The Main Mash and Fermentation

With a completed yeast starter, the brewer has a crop of pure, vigorous sake yeast, raring to get on with the primary business of alcoholic fermentation. Steamed rice, kōji, and water are added to the starter, by the process called mashing, in three stages over four days, doubling the volume and reducing the temperature of the mash at each stage. Nowadays, we know that these are sophisticated biotechnological techniques to prevent spoilage; that the craftsmen of the Middle Ages came to this conclusion without technology seems almost miraculous.

The main alcoholic fermentation lasts from a couple of weeks to well over a month, depending on the grade of sake and other factors. The pattern of fermentation in sake brewing is unique and complex, and is technically distinguished from simpler systems by the name multiple parallel fermentation.

The first addition roughly halves the acidity and density of yeast in the mash. The second day is a rest period called *odori*, during which the yeast grows back to almost the concentrations of the original starter. The second and third additions take place on successive days, so the whole mashing period takes four days. The standard system of mashing in three stages is called *san-dan-jikomi*.

The Drama of Fermentation

Once all the ingredients have gone into the tank on day four, the rice absorbs the water. After a few hours, there is no liquid visible on the surface of what becomes a great, inert, glistening dome of rice. Throughout the fermentation period, brewers stir the mash morning and evening with long, flat-headed paddles. At first, the mash is so stiff that it is a day or two before the paddles can be forced through. Enzymes from the kōji gradually dissolve the rice, making the mash more liquid. The density of the mash and the low temperature work as brakes on the activity of the yeast, so the first few days see a build up of sugars before it gets up to speed in converting them to alcohol. After a couple of days, the surface begins to crack as the mash loosens and the yeast begins to work. Strings of lacy bubbles appear over the ruptures like lava welling from fissures on the slopes of a volcano. The foam spreads from the first cracks, covering the mash first in a light, frothy layer, then, after a week or so, a meter-high mass of thick, creamy bubbles. Once this foam drops back, the contents of the tank seem to be on the point of eruption for several days. Startling waves well through the mash as if something were alive in there. Something is alive in there, of course, though nothing like the sea-serpent the surging movements suggest. The surges are caused by the enormous amounts of carbon dioxide gas created in the soupy mash by the yeast as fermentation reaches top speed. After the foam has disappeared completely, the surface of the mash seethes with small bubbles. As the yeast moves into the home stretch, the fireworks subside, and the telltale bubbles become fewer and fewer. The brewer begins to consider pressing. In days past, tōji handled the mash and judged the timing of pressing using only their senses and experience, with taste, smell, and the consistency of the foam as a guide. Nowadays, these skills are supplemented by chemical analysis. If the mash is too young, the sake will suffer from off-flavors and be unstable in storage. Left too long, the yeast dies off in the mash, causing rough flavors and unpleasant aromas.

Optional Extras before Pressing

Additions—When the brewer is working in the pure-rice style, we proceed with no delay. With lower grades of sake, or alcohol-added Premium Sake, the additions are made at this point, before pressing. A dash of alcohol added to the fermenting mash traps in the volatile fragrances that are so easily lost.

Fourth addition—Mashing is carried out in three stages. Sometimes, there is a fourth stage shortly before pressing, designed to make the sake sweeter or deeper in flavor, and to boost yield.

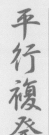

Multiple Parallel Fermentation: Making the Right Stuff the Hard Way

"Chemistry is a mystery, just like ancient history."—The Nolans

People have found ways of making stimulating alcoholic drinks since time immemorial, beginning long before there were methods to record such matters. Evidence shows that whatever materials Nature provided were used to advantage: fruits, such as grapes and apples; grains, including rice and barley; and even less likely candidates such as tree sap and mare's milk. Over the past couple of hundred years, it has become clear that all the excellent and intoxicating concoctions produced have resulted from sugar being converted to alcohol by yeast.

Although indications are that people were making a type of beer four thousand years ago, authorities generally believe that wine represents mankind's first alcoholic achievement. This is because the pattern of fermentation that leads to wine is simplicity itself, and technically it is called just that: simple fermentation.

Grapes are sweet because their juice is more than twenty percent glucose. Add some cooperative yeast, and away you go. Since yeast is naturally present in the skin of grapes, this poses no problem—at least for those who live where grapes grow.

For those who must concoct something from grain, such as barley, the challenge is greater. The aspiring brewer must find a way of turning the starch (the raw material of the grain) into sugar. In the natural world, barley grains produce an enzyme that converts starch to a sugar (maltose) because the plant needs energy to put out shoots and to reproduce. The crafty brewer, meanwhile, roasts the barley before it shoots, trapping the sugar in the grain. The product is then cooked to make a sugary soup, yeast is thrown in, and presto: one has all the ingredients to make everyone happy. Multiple fermentation is the term used to denote the two consecutive stages (making sugar, turning it into alcohol) of beer brewing.

Sake fermentation also has multiple stages. However, whereas the two stages are separate and consecutive in beer brewing, they occur simultaneously in sake making. Kōji enzymes continually produce sugars during the weeks in which the rice is left to ferment, while yeast simultaneously converts the enzymes to alcohol. Sake brewing is akin to walking a tightrope: the two elements must be perfectly balanced.

Since the production of sugars and their consumption is simultaneous, the total quantity of sugars produced can be very large indeed. Thus, were all that sugar made at once, in beer-like fashion, the sheer density of sugar would stifle the yeast. It is up to the skilled sake maker to ensure that the sugars are released gradually, allowing the tōji to brew to produce a higher alcohol content than would otherwise be possible.

▶ Fermenting sake with a full head of foam. The texture, timing, and aroma of the foam all provide clues to the brewer as to the state of the sake, and how to handle the fermentation.

STAGE 5 · Pressing

Finally, the brewer presses the sake, separating the liquid from the remaining rice and kōji solids. Most breweries now use automatic pressing machinery, although in places there remains an arduous older system of pressing the mash after pouring it into hundreds of small bags.

Machine Press

The automatic press is made up of a series of boards assembled in a strong frame, each board sheathed in a mesh of synthetic material. The boards are pressed shut by a hydraulic ram, to form a large pressing chamber with cavities between. The mash is pumped into the cavities, and balloon-like attachments are inflated, pressing the solids into sheets. The clear liquid sake passes through the mesh coverings and flows out the bottom. When the batch has been fully pressed, the caked solids (*kasu*) are removed from the boards. One pressing cycle happens within twenty-four hours.

Traditional Press

The traditional system for hand pressing sake uses bags about 28 by 10 inches (70 by 25 centimeters), stacked in a long, deep, rectangular receptacle. The *moromi* is poured or pumped into the individual bags, which are then laid in an alternating pattern at the bottom of the press (*fune*). When stacking is finished, the result resembles a waterbed comprising hundreds of individual bags. The bags have to be restacked before pressing can be completed, so this old-fashioned system requires more labor and time—at least a day more than the modern machine press.

Pressure-Free Pressing

The greater the pressure applied during pressing, the more sake is produced. However, brewers know that the quality of sake gained at high pressure suffers. Conversely, the fact that low pressure means better sake finds its technical expression in the method called *fukuro-tsuri*—literally, bag-hanging. The mash is poured into bags such as those used with the traditional press, and strung up to hang. (This has given rise to the brewer's black humor in the expression, *kubi-tsuri*, referring to being hung by the neck by the hangman.) Only the sake that drips out under its own weight is collected, usually in 4-gallon (18-liter) bottles called *tobin*. Only a very small amount of this *shizuku* sake is produced by this labor-intensive method, so its use is often restricted to the production of sake destined for entry in the national trade contest in spring.

STAGE 6 · Treatment after Pressing

After pressing has finished, the brewer must keep the sake in good condition until it is ready for bottling and sale. The clear liquid which flows out of the bottom of the press is collected in tanks. Fermentation as such has stopped, but the brewer's worries are not yet over: The sake is still unstable. Depending on the sake, there may still be some live yeast. Enzyme action continues, and the brewer must ensure that lactic acid bacteria are not present in sufficient quantity to cause dam-

age. Freshly pressed sake is unpasteurized, with a high percentage of alcohol. Called *nama genshu*, it sometimes finds its way to the consumer almost or completely untouched, but sake generally undergoes filtration, pasteurization, dilution, and the removal of sediment.

Removing pressed lees from the boards of the machine press.

1. Removal of Sediment

After a few days in the tank, enzyme- and yeast-heavy sediment (*ori*) settles on the bottom. This mix of solids influences the flavor of the sake, and blocks filters, so it is usually siphoned off mechanically, a task known as *ori-biki*. (This stage may be omitted if there is little sediment, as is often the case with machine-pressed sake.)

2. Filtration of New Sake

Mechanical filtration through carbon is standard. There are degrees of filtration, from rough filtering, which only aims to remove minute solid particles, to ultra-filtration, which is fine enough to eliminate enzymes that alter sake flavor during storage. This system is used by larger companies to make unpasteurized sake safer to handle. Small amounts of sake are sold unfiltered.

3. Pasteurization

By raising the temperature to above 140° F (60° C), the brewer can stop enzyme action, and kill off the feared lactic acid bacteria that spoil sake. Small breweries tend to accomplish this by pumping the sake through a spiral pipe, immersed in hot water. Heat exchangers are a more sophisticated option.

4. Storage/Maturation

The classic kan-zukuri (cold-weather brewing) pattern of sake production concentrates the season in the chilliest months. The traditional rhythm was to brew through the winter, then pasteurize all the new sake in spring for safe storage through the summer. The tanks were left, sealed and untouched, through the hottest months, when spoiling micro organisms thrive most easily. This is still the standard practice, the new sake being stored in sealed enamel or stainless steel tanks, before making its debut on the market, suitably rounded and matured, in autumn. The traditional pattern of sake being brewed and consumed in a one-and-a-bit year cycle is still prevalent, but it has diversified as growing quantities of sake are sold increasingly younger, as shiboritate (fresh-pressed) or nama (unpasteurized) sake, or increasingly older, as aged sake (jukuseishu or koshu).

5. Treatment before Shipping

The standard system sees sake filtered and pasteurized once more before being diluted and bottled, ready for shipping.

GLOSSARY

acidity: key element of flavor. The acidity of sake reflects the quantity of organic acids (lactic acid, succinic acid, and so on) present.

aged sake: See *koshu* and *jukuseishu*

aji ginjō 味吟醸: See *ginjō*

aka chōchin 赤ちょうちん: "Red lantern." Red paper lanterns are hung outside inexpensive eating and drinking establishments in Japan, and the name of the lanterns indicates the hostelries themselves by extension.

alcohol-added sake: sake fortified with neutral brewers' alcohol, added to the mash before pressing.

amai, amakuchi 甘い, 甘口: sweet

amino acids: important elements contributing to body and *umami* flavor (q.v.). Sake is extremely rich in amino acids.

ashifumi seimai 足踏み精米: old rice-polishing method, using man-powered pestles raised by stepping on one end of a long wooden lever.

atsu-kan あつ燗: hot sake

ato-aji 後味: aftertaste

cask sake: See *taru-zake*

chinmi 珍味: drinkers' snacks and delicacies

choko 猪口, ちょこ: small sake cups

Chūgoku 中国: the western leg of the main Honshū island, framed by Tottori and Okayama prefectures on one side and Yamaguchi on the far western end.

chūhai 酎ハイ: popular drink made from *shōchū* spirit with fruit and other flavorings.

cloudy sake: See *nigori-zake* and *ori-zake*

dai ginjō 大吟醸: the highest grade of sake, made from white rice polished to 50 percent or less of its original size.

fugu-fin sake: See *hire-zake*

fukumi-ka 含み香: "flavor-in-the-mouth." The range of fragrances that fill the palate after sake is taken into the mouth (as opposed to *uwadachi-ka*, the aromas detected with the nose before drinking). Also called *kōchū-ka* (lit. "fragrance in the mouth").

fukurami ふくらみ: lit. "expansiveness." A taster's word to describe the blossoming of a good sake's flavor on the palate.

fukuro-shibori 袋しぼり: the traditional system for pressing sake in bags (*fukuro*). Laborious and requiring a certain amount of experience to get right, but still hanging on in places. The first, cloudy sake to trickle from the press under its own weight is called *arabashiri*. After minute particles of rice solids have formed a natural filter, clear *nakagumi* sake flows for several hours. Finally, a heavy lid is lowered onto the bags, and pressure is applied. The bags are restacked for the final stage of pressing. The last sake yielded is called *seme*.

fukuro-zuri 袋吊り: a laborious, low-yield process of pressing sake without applying pressure. The mash is hung up in bags, and only the tiny portion of the sake that drips out under its own weight is collected. The resulting sake is known as *shizuku*.

genshu 原酒: undiluted sake

ginjō 吟醸: high-grade "special brew sake." Tends to the fruity and fragrant, and must be made of highly polished white rice.

   aji-ginjō: the style of *ginjō* brewing that lays emphasis on structure of taste rather than on a flowery fragrance.

   kaori-ginjō: the opposite of *aji-ginjō*: the school of thought that stresses a prominent fragrance.

ginjō-ka 吟醸香: the fruity, flowery fragrance associated with *ginjō* sake.

ginjōshu 吟醸酒: see *ginjō* (*shu* is a reading of the char-acter for sake, so this term means the same as *ginjō*).

ginjō-zukuri 吟醸造り: the techniques used when making *ginjō* sake

-gō (suffix) 合: a unit of volume, equivalent to 180 ml, or 6 fl. oz. Traditional Japanese measures are widely used alongside metric units, and are themselves in fact logically arranged in multiples of ten. Thus, ten *gō* equal one *sho* (that is 1.8 liters/60 oz.), one large bottle of sake), and ten of those make one *to* (eighteen liters). Though this is already out of the range of most drinkers' imaginations, there is also the *koku* (180 liters), still widely used by brewery folk when talking about production capacity.

guinomi ぐいのみ, ぐい呑み: a large sake cup

hanami 花見: flower viewing and related festivities

happō-sei seishu 発泡性清酒: See *sparkling sake*

heiko fukuhakko 平行複発酵: see *multiple parallel fermentation*

hi-ire 火入れ: pasteurization. By heating to around 149° F (65° C), brewers stop enzyme and yeast action to stabilize flavor, and kill off spoiling lactic acid bacteria, the brewer's worst fear.

hire-zake ひれ酒: *fugu*-fin sake. Sake infused with the smoked fin of the blowfish (*fugu*) to give a distinctive smoky, fishy flavor.

hito-hada 人肌: literally "people's skin," this term refers to sake served at body temperature, just slightly warm.

Hokuriku 北陸: a string of four prefectures in central Honshū from Niigata to Fukui prefectures that runs along the northern coast fronting the Japan Sea.

honjōzō 本醸造: "Free brew sake." Premium Sake category. *Honjōzō* sake is made with rice polished to 70 percent or less of original size, with a limited addition of brewers' alcohol.

hon-nama 本生: See *nama chozōshu*

Honshū 本州: the largest of Japan's four main islands.

ippanmai 一般米: "regular rice." Brewers' expression for ordinary table rice when used to make sake. (Also referred to as *hanmai*, roughly "eating rice.")

isshō-bin 一升瓶: the big 1.8-liter (60-ounce) bottles

izakaya 居酒屋: nearest English equivalent is "pub," but *izakaya* are all about eating as well as drinking.

ja no me 蛇の目: snake's eye. The name of the pattern made by the concentric circles at the bottom of a sake tasting cup.

ji-zake 地酒: a term often used, but rarely defined. Written with characters meaning "sake of the country," it has wide currency as a kind of code for authentic sake. Variously rendered by suffering translators as "regional sake," "local sake," "country sake," and so on.

jō-on 常温: room temperature

jukusei-ka 熟成香: pleasant aromas of aged sake

jukuseishu 熟成酒: aged sake (lit. matured sake)

junmai 純米: "pure rice." See *junmaishu*

junmai ginjō 純米吟醸: A grade of Premium Sake. Made with rice, *kōji*, and water alone, from white rice polished to 60 percent or less of its original size.

junmaishu 純米酒: "pure-rice sake." One of the Premium categories of sake. "*Junmai* type" is sometimes used to indicate all sakes made from rice and water alone, even *junmai ginjō* and *junmai dai ginjō* (which are higher grades than *junmaishu*).

-ka (suffix) 香: Written with the character 香 meaning fragrance, this occurs in many compound words relating to sake (*ginjō-ka*, *jukusei-ka*, etc.).

kaiseki ryōri 懐石料理: a formal style of Japanese dining, originally closely associated with the tea ceremony.

kanpai 乾杯: Japanese for cheers

kan-zake 燗酒: heated sake

kan-zukuri 寒造り: "cold-brewing." Refers to the system in which brewing was restricted to the coldest months of winter, which was established in the Edo Period (1600–1868), and remains the base of contemporary brewing practice.

kaori ginjō 香り吟醸: See *ginjō*

karai, karakuchi 辛い, 辛口: dry

kashira 頭: written with the character for *head*, the *kashira* in a traditional brewery is the master brewer's right hand, supervising the practical everyday details of brewing.

kasu かす, 粕: the solid cake of leftover rice solids which remains after pressing. Rich in vitamins, it is used in making Japanese pickles, and is a valued ingredient in Japanese cooking.

katakuchi かたくち, 片口: open-mouthed decanters for pouring sake

keg sake: See *taru-zake*

kijōshu 貴醸酒: sake which is made by replacing a portion of the brewing water with sake. The method has its roots in antique brewing methods.

kiki choko 利き猪口, 利きちょこ: tasting cup, usually made of white porcelain with pattern of two cobalt blue concentric circles to make the show the clarity and color of the sake more clearly.

kiki-zake 利き酒: sake tasting

kimoto 生酛: the main system for producing the yeast starter from the eighteenth century, more time-consuming and nerve-wracking than "quick-fermenting," which became the standard into the twentieth century.

Kinki 近畿: the west-central section of the main Honshū island that includes Hyōgo, Osaka, Kyoto, Shiga, Wakayama, Mie, and Nara prefectures.

kōbo 酵母: yeast (written in Japanese with characters indicating "the mother of fermentation").

kodaishu 古代酒: lit., "sake of antiquity." Refers to the genre of products made to varying degree of authenticity using old methods.

kōji 麹: the mold at the heart of sake brewing. Its proper name is Aspergillus oryzae, and it produces a variety of enzymes while growing on steamed rice. These have the cumulative effect of denaturalizing rice starch to make fermentable sugars.

kome 米: rice

koshiki こし器, 濾し器: the pot used for steaming rice in traditional brewing.

koshu 古酒: aged sake

kura 蔵: Also *sakagura*. A sake brewery. Traditional storehouse buildings are also called *kura*, but this is usually written with a different character.

kurabito 蔵人: "brewery person." Refers to the brewery workers under the leadership of the *tōji* (master brewer).

kuramoto 蔵元: a brewery owner. With a very different ring from Japanese terms indicating general ownership, or the proprietors of a business generally, the term suggests the scion of a deep-rooted family firm—as most sake breweries are.

kyōkai kōbo 協会酵母: Association yeast. Yeast strains maintained and distributed by the Brewer's Association of Japan, which are in wide use.

low-alcohol sake: has anywhere from a beer-like 4 or 5 percent alcohol to a winey range of 12 or 13. An increasingly popular genre in this age of "light drinks" where the 15-to-16 percent alcohol of standard products seems a little heavy to many consumers.

masu ます, 枡: a peculiarly charming square wooden box that now serves as a sake cup mainly on festive occasions.

modori-ka 戻り香: lit. "returning fragrance." Refers to the range of fragrances that linger after sake has been swallowed.

moromi もろみ, 醪: fermenting sake mash

multiple parallel fermentation: the complicated sake fermentation system, in which the conversion of starch into sugar and that of sugar into alcohol happens simultaneously in the mash.

mu-roka 無濾過: "unfiltered." Sake is filtered twice in the commonest system, but single filtration, or even completely unfiltered sake, has become more common.

mu-roka nama genshu 無濾過生原酒: unfiltered, unpasteurized, undiluted sake—exactly as it came out of the press.

Nada: the most prolific brewing region, located on the coast of Hyōgo Prefecture. Its coastal location was one of a number of factors in its rise, as the handy port facilities made it easy for the Nada breweries to get their products to the thirsty market of the Tokyo capital (still known as Edo when Nada first reached the top of the sake ladder in the eighteenth century).

nama 生: written with the character meaning raw or live, it means unpasteurized in the case of sake.

nama chozōshu 生貯蔵酒: *chozō* means storage, so *nama chozō* (often colloquially shortened to *nama-cho*) means sake that was stored unpasteurized. Sake is most commonly pasteurized twice, once before storage, and once again before shipping. *Nama-chozō* aims to retain the characteristic freshness of completely unpasteurized *hon-nama* (or *nama-nama*) sake, while avoiding the storage problems of "live" sake.

nama genshu 生原酒: sake which is unpasteurized and undiluted

nama-nama 生生: see *nama chozōshu*

nama-zake 生酒: unpasteurized sake

National Assessment for New Sake: understated title for a high-powered event. Now held under the auspices of the National Brewing Research Institute, in Hiroshima. Breweries from all Japan submit their finest *dai ginjō* brews of the season to the scrutiny of the judges in the quest for a prestigious Gold Medal. Winning brews are sometimes marketed as such (labeled "Gold Medal Sake," *kinshō shu*).

nigori-zake にごり酒, 濁り酒: "cloudy sake." *Nigori* contains rice solids in suspension. These settle to the bottom of the bottle during storage, and the sake is usually shaken and drunk in a milky white state. A minor, though durable genre in Japan, *nigori* is tremendously popular in the United States.

nihonshudo 日本酒度: See *sake meter value*

"noble brew sake": See *kijōshu*

nodogoshi のどごし, 喉ごし: the feel of a sake on the way down. Sake tasters also talk about *shita-zawari* (how a sake feels on the tongue) and *kuchi-atari* (lit. "how it hits the mouth"); indicates the texture of the sake on the palate and the whole mouth).

non-premium sake: see *regular sake*

nuka ぬか, 糠: rice powder, the waste product left after rice polishing

nuru-kan ぬる燗: warm sake (as opposed to hot *atsukan*)

o-kan おかん, お燗: the common honorific term for warmed sake

o-kan-ki お燗器: machines for heating sake

ori おり, 滓: the fine lees left after pressing sake, especially with the traditional *fune* press. As the lees are rich in yeast and active enzymes, they are usually quickly removed by a siphoning process (called *ori-biki*) to improve flavor stability. Sometimes they are deliberately left when making a variety of *nigori-zake* called *ori-zake*.

ori-zake おり酒, 滓酒: See *ori*

o-shaku お酌: the custom of pouring and being poured for as an integral part of sake drinking.

otoko-zake 男酒: "masculine sake." Refers to punchy,

dry sake. Most commonly associated with the dry brews of Nada (q.v.).

Premium Sake: used in this book as an equivalent to the Japanese Tokutei Meishōshu (特定名称酒, "Special Designation Sake"). Category includes *junmai*, *honjōzō*, *ginjō*, *junmai ginjō*, *dai ginjō*, and *junmai dai ginjō*.

pure-rice sake: See *junmaishu*

regular sake: humbler sake, which doesn't qualify for a Premium ranking.

reishu 冷酒: chilled sake

rice-polishing: a kind of milling process, removing the outer (brown) part of the rice grain before use in brewing.

rice-polishing ratio: given as a percentage, representing the amount of the original grain of rice (remaining after polishing) used in brewing. A part of the definition of some high grades, and a key factor in the production cost and quality of sake.

sae さえ, 冴え: taster's word for clarity of sake

sakamai 酒米: colloquial brewer's term for *shuzo kotekimai*

sakana 肴: food to go with sake

sakazuki さかずき, 盃, 杯: a sake cup

sake meter: the hydrometer (used to measure sake's specific gravity) which is marked with gradations showing plus and minus figures. Though the sake meter value (see following entry) is used as a rule of thumb to indicate the sweetness or dryness of a sake, the specific gravity is not entirely determined by sugar content. This fact, combined with the effect of levels of acids and amino acids on the perceived flavor, means that experienced drinkers tend to shunt the SMV ever further down their lists of things to think about when considering sake.

sake meter value (SMV): a measure of sake sweetness, indicated with plus or minus before a number. Nominally, plus is dry, and minus is sweet. (Zero is theoretically neither sweet nor dry, though most contemporary palates perceive sake with an SMV of zero as on the sweet side.) The larger the number, the drier (or sweeter) the sake. See also *sake meter*.

sake nouveau: See *shinshu* and *shiboritate*

sanzōshu 三増酒: See *triple sake*

seed mash: See *yeast starter*

seimai 精米: See *rice-polishing*

seimai buai 精米歩合: See *rice-polishing ratio*

shibori しぼり, 搾り: pressing. The process of removing remaining solids to give clear sake.

shibori-tate しぼりたて, 搾りたて: "freshly pressed" sake

shibui 渋い: astringent (adjectival form of *shibumi*; see following entry)

shibumi 渋み: astringency. An unfortunate-sounding word in English, but a key element of the balance of taste, akin to the tannic elements intrinsic to red wine flavor.

shikomi しこみ, 仕込み: the mashing process

shinshu 新酒: new sake

Shinto: the animistic religion which quietly informs many areas of Japanese life. Sake brewers offer sake to the sake divinity at key points in the season.

shizuku 滴: Also *shizuku-zake*. Sake made by the pressure-free *fukuro-zuri* method (q.v.).

-shō (suffix) 升: See *gō*

shōchū 焼酎: Japanese spirit, distinguished by use of *kōji* in initial fermentation stage.

shōkōshu 紹興酒: fermented Chinese beverage

shubo 酒母: Also called *moto*. The yeast starter. Sake brewing has had a separate process solely to propagate yeast since the Middle Ages.

shuzō 酒造: brewing (or brewery). Frequently occurs as part of company name, e.g. Honolulu Shuzō (Honolulu Sake Brewery).

shuzō kōtekimai 酒造好適米: true brewers' rice.

Colloquially called *sakamai* (sake rice) by brewers.

sparking sake: bubbly sake

special brew sake: See *ginjō*

starter mash: See *yeast starter*

tanrei karakuchi 淡麗辛口: describes a light, dry, crisp drinking style associated strongly with sake from Niigata Prefecture in the minds of many sake fans.

taru 樽: wooden keg or cask. Now generally used only to store and serve sake on high days and holidays, though some deliberately wood-scented sake is sold as *taru-zake* (see following entry). A small group of producers have resurrected the practice of actually brewing in wooden vessels in the last few years, but almost all sake is now fermented in enamel-lined or stainless tanks.

taru-zake 樽酒: sake that is briefly aged in wooden casks to give wood fragrance and flavor to the final product.

tei-arukōru shu 低アルコール酒: See low-alcohol sake

teri てり, 照り: taster's word for the brilliant clarity of sake

tobin 斗瓶: an 18-liter bottle, often used to store *shizuku* sake intended for entry into the national contest for new sake. See also *gō*.

Tōhoku 東北: region covering the entire north end of the main island of Honshū, from Fukushima Prefecture in the south to Aomori at the north end.

tōji 杜氏: a master brewer

tōji seido 杜氏制度: the *tōji* system, the traditional system of manpower for sake brewing centered on the seasonally active craftsmen of the regional brewers' guilds.

tokkuri とっくり, 徳利: the little decanters used to serve and, especially, heat, sake.

tokubetsu 特別: "special." Prefixed to *junmai* and *honjōzō* to designate confusing sub-genres.

triple sake: regular sake made by adding brewers' alcohol, sugars, and organic acids to the original sake to triple the volume. Originally developed in the times of scarcity associated with World War Two, this economical but widely criticized genre looks set to be relegated to a minor role, if not eliminated by upcoming changes in tax law.

"true brew sake": See *honjōzō*

tsukimi 月見: moon viewing and associated festivities

tsumami つまみ: bits and pieces of food to go with sake (or other drinks, at a pinch). Usually used in honorific form *o-tsumami*.

umami うまみ, 旨み: freed at last from having to explain that this is untranslatable, as it gains currency as an English loan word. *Umami* has been recognized as a basic flavor (like sweet, sour, bitter, etc.). Originally pinned down as the key flavor element in Japanese *dashi* fish stock, tomatoes and parmesan cheese have also been found to be rich in *umami* flavor. For sake drinkers, it is the rich, full, satisfying flavor (almost texture) deriving from rice, and deepening with time.

undiluted sake: See *genshu*

unfiltered sake: See *mu-roka*

unpasteurized sake: See *nama-zake* and *nama chozōshu*

uwadachi-ka 上立ち香: "top nose." The volatile fragrances that are detectable from the surface of sake, before drinking.

yamahai 山廃: complex traditional system for making the yeast starter (adapted from *kimoto*; q.v.). Refers by extension to sake made using this method.

yeast starter (also starter mash, seed mash): a separate stage in brewing, specifically for the purpose of propagating sake yeast. The two major schools are the *sokujō* (quick-fermenting) school and its variants, and the *kimoto* school, comprising the original *kimoto* method and the revised *yamahai* system.

-zake (suffix) 酒: equals "sake"

INDEX

SAKE SPECS

Name	Brand Name	Brewery	Page	Rice Variety
Ama no To, Umashine	Ama no To	Asamai Shuzō	36	Gin no Sei, Miyama Nishiki
Biwa no Chōju, Dai Ginjō	Biwa no Chōju	Ikemoto Shuzō	40	Tama-sakae, Yamada Nishiki
Chikuha, Dai Ginjō	Chikuha	Kazuma Shuzō	19	Yamada Nishiki
Dai Ginjō, Gold Kamotsuru	Kamotsuru	Kamotsuru Shuzō	77	Yamada Nishiki, etc.
Daishichi, Junmai Kimoto	Daishichi	Daishichi Shuzō	43	Gohyakuman-goku
Dassai, Junmai Ginjō, 45 Nama-zake	Dassai	Asahi Shuzō	42	Yamada Nishiki
Denshu, Tokubetsu Junmaishu	Denshu	Nishida Shuzō-ten	58	Hanafubuki
Eikō Fuji, Ginjō Shōnai-Homare	Shōnai-Homare, Eikō Fuji,	Fuji Shuzō	86	Miyama Nishiki
Eikun, Dai Ginjō, Iroha	Eikun	Eikun Shuzō	65	Yamada Nishiki
Fukuchō Saya, Ginjō	Fukuchō	Imada Shuzō	76	Yamada Nishiki
Funaguchi Kikusui, Ichiban-shibori, Honjōzō Nama Genshu	Kikusui	Kikusui Shuzō	42	
Gokyō, Ginjō Genshu	Gokyō	Sakai Shuzō	44	Yamada Nishiki
Hanahato Kijōshu, 7-nen Chozō	Hanahato	Enoki Shuzō	50	Nakate shinsenbon
Hōhōshu	Kamo Midori, Chikurin	Marumoto Shuzō	51	Akebono
Ichi no Kura, Himezen	Ichi no Kura	Ichi no Kura	45	Toyo Nishiki, etc.
Ippongi Junmaishu	Ippongi	Ippongi Kubo Honten	83	Gohyakuman-goku
Izumibashi, Tokubetsu Junmaishu	Izumibashi	Izumibashi Shuzō	36	Yamada Nishiki (from Kanagawa)
Junmai Dai Ginjō, Kame no O	Kiyoizumi	Kusumi Shuzō	83	Kame no O
Junmai Dai Ginjō, Sanka	Masumi	Miyasaka Jōzō	41	Yamada Nishiki
Junmai Ginjō, Momo no Shizuku	Momo no Shizuku	Matsumoto Shuzō	71	Gohyakuman-goku
Junmai Ginjō, Shukon	Tama no Hikari	Tama no Hikari Shuzō	43	Yamada Nishiki, Nihonbare, etc.
Kaden Ginjōshu	Mado no Ume	Mado no Ume Shuzō	39	Saikai 134
Kaiun, Dai Ginjō	Kaiun	Doi Shuzō-jō	64	Yamada Nishiki
Kamitaka, Dai Ginjō	Kamitaka	Eigashima Shuzō	73	Yamada Nishiki
Kamoshibito Kuheiji, Mu-roka Warimizu Nashi	Kamoshibito Kuheiji	Banjō Jōzō	48	Yamada Nishiki
Kasumochi Genshu, Yauemonshu	Yauemonshu, Yamatogawa	Yamatogawa Shuzō-ten	44	Gohyakuman-goku
Kenbishi	Kenbishi	Kenbishi Shuzō	49	
Kikuhide, Dai Ginjō Kura	Kikuhide	Kitsukura Shuzō	67	Miyama Nishiki, Yamada Nishiki
Kinmatsu Hakutaka, Tokubetsu Junmai	Haku Taka	Hakutaka	80	Yamada Nishiki
Kirin Hizōshu	Kirin	Kaetsu Shuzō	46	Yamada Nishiki
Kodaimai-zukuri, Asamurasaki	Kikusakari	Kiuchi Shuzō	51	Gohyakuman-goku, Asamurasaki Genmai
Kokuryū, Junmai Ginjō	Kokuryū	Kokuryū Shuzō	39	Gohyakuman-goku
Koshi no Kanbai, Bessen, Tokubetsu Honjōzō	Koshi no Kanbai	Ishimoto Shuzō	37	Gohyakuman-goku
Masuizumi, Junmai Dai Ginjō	Masuizumi	Masuda Shuzō-ten	41	Yamada Nishiki
Miyo-zakura Shibori-tate, Tokubetsu Junmai	Miyo-zakura	Miyo-zakura Jōzō	45	Miyama Nishiki
Momotose 1972	Fukumitsuya	Fukumitsuya	46	Gohyakuman-goku
Naruto Tai, Junmai Ginjō Genshu	Naruto Tai	Honke Matsuura Shuzō-jō	74	Gohyakuman-goku
Ōka Ginjōshu	Dewazakura	Dewazakura Shuzō	39	Miyama Nishiki, Yuki Geshō
Oku no Matsu, Tokubetsu Junmaishu	Oku no Matsu	Oku no Matsu Shuzō	36	Rice from Fukushima Pref.
Ōnakaya, Junmai Dai Ginjō	Shichiken	Yamanashi Meijō	41	Yamada Nishiki
Rihaku, Junmai Ginjō, Chōtokusen	Rihaku	Rihaku Shuzō	75	Yamada Nishiki
Rikyūbai, Junmai Dai Ginjō	Rikyūbai	Daimon Shuzō	41	Yamada Nishiki
Sawa no I, Junmai Dai-karakuchi	Sawa no I	Ozawa Shuzō	63	Akebono, Nihonbare
Seishu Hakkaisan	Hakkaisan	Hakkai Jōzō	49	Gohyakuman-goku, Yuki no Sei
Suehiro, Honjōzō Kira	Suehiro	Suehiro Shuzō	37	Gohyakuman-goku
Takashimizu, Seisen Karakuchi	Takashimizu	Akita Shurui Seizō	49	Rice from Akita Pref.
Tatsuriki, Dai Ginjō, Kome no Sasayaki	Tatsuriki	Honda Shōten	81	Yamada Nishiki
Tokubetsu Junmai, Kin Taruhei	Taruhei	Taruhei Shuzō	51	Yamada Nishiki
Tsuki no Katsura, Nakakumi Nigori-zake	Tsuki no Katsura	Masuda Tokubei Shōten	47	Gohyakuman-goku, Nihonbare
Ume no Yado, Bizen Omachi, Junmai Dai Ginjō	Ume no Yado	Ume no Yado Shuzō	82	Bizen Omachi
Urakasumi Zen	Urakasumi	Saura	39	Toyo Nishiki
Yamahai Junmaishu, Hiraizumi	Hiraizumi	Hiraizumi Honpo	59	Miyama Nishiki
Yoshinogawa, Dai Ginjō	Yoshinogawa	Yoshinogawa	67	Gohyakuman-goku